Times Remen

Growing Up in Killamarsh

&

A Village History

A Peek into the Past

Times Remembered

Growing Up in Killamarsh

&

A Village History

A Peek into the Past

Bernard Dye
with support from K. Warnes
and members of Killamarsh Tenants & Residents Forum

© Bernard Dye

Published by Killamarsh Tenants & Residents Forum 2010

14 Stanley Street
Killamarsh
Sheffield
S21 1EL

ISBN 978-0-9565852-0-2

Prepared and printed by:

Pasttimes Publishing Ltd
64 Hallfield Road
Layerthorpe
York YO31 7ZQ
Tel: 01904 431213

Website: www.pasttimespublishing.co.uk

Contents

A Village History

Acknowledgements

Rykneld Homes, especially David Street for support and funding.

Councillor Alan Charles, Derbyshire County Council for support and funding.

North East Derbyshire District Council and Arts Officers Kay Ogilvie and Helena Davenport for supporting this project from its beginnings with a Small Arts Grant. Aileen and Vincent Hopkinson for help in research.

Matlock Records Office for help in research.

Chesterfield Museum and curator Anne-Marie Knowles for help with research.

Pamela Butler for her invaluable help in all stages of the preparation of the book.

Federation of Tenants for their support and advice.

Links CVS of Chesterfield for advice on funding.

And of course, Killamarsh Tenant and Residents Forum for giving me the confidence I needed to continue when things were proving difficult.

Last but not least, David Clark for all his help and being there at the start. Apologies to anyone I have inadvertently missed.

My eternal thanks to you all.

Bernard Dye

Times Remembered

Growing up in Killamarsh

1. My arrival

My arrival in Killamarsh was brought about by the following events, I was born in 1928 on the 10th of November in a row of houses on Stirrup Road near the village of Oldcoates close to the town of Worksop in Nottinghamshire.

My father's name was William Dye milkman of Oldcoates. He married my mother, Sarah Jane Evans of Kiveton which is a village three miles north of Killamarsh. In all my mother bore eight children myself being the eighth. Six months after my birth my mum died at the age of 36. During her illness the man who was my father was having an affair with a woman by the name of Emily Corkill.

After my mother's death my father married this woman and such was the trust she had in his fidelity, she would accompany him on his morning milk-round. To do this, both of them would tie my brother Leslie and myself to our bed, but unknown to them, my sisters Doris and Florence would sneak away from the farm where they worked and untie us, but they were obliged to tie us back up before father and stepmother returned from their milk deliveries, for my sisters' safety as well as ours.

**Mum
Sarah Jane Evans.**

This and other cruelties which I will not dwell upon resulted in my brother and I being placed in a care home by the authorities. Where this home was I cannot discover, much to my sorrow as I have tried to no avail.

My eldest brother Billy had joined the navy as a boy sailor at the age of 14. When he reached adulthood he discovered our plight and contacted members of the Evans family as well as his siblings.

So one morning, I was aged just over 5 years and Leslie was 8 years old, I remember being dressed in my sailor suit, then Leslie and I were placed on a train in the guard's van. We knew nothing of what was going on, only that we were under orders not to leave the guard's van until we were told. I remember that the guard gave us a cup of tea which to us was undrinkable as it was so strong, but he eventually saw his error and gave us a drink of milk.

We arrived at this station, which I now know to be the Sheffield Midland. The guard tidied us up a little then took us onto the platform, where, after the other passengers had dispersed we saw two ladies still on the platform.

How do I describe these ladies? I must resort to my thoughts as a young boy. One of the ladies was tall and slim, I thought she was beautiful. Now about the other lady, please do not think that I am being insulting but this is the only way I can describe her, she was not very tall in fact she was so short the only picture I as a boy can paint is that she looked square. Anyway these two ladies rushed up to us, the tall one grabbed Leslie and the square lady grabbed me and pressed me to her ample bosom and I thought my time had come as I struggled to breathe.

That was the first meeting with my Aunt Mary the square one, or Polly as she was fondly known. The tall lady turned out to be my eldest sister Edith who took Leslie and brought him up on the Manor estate in Killamarsh.

So that meeting on that dirty, smelly railway station proved to be the turning point of my life. You see it was from that moment I was with my Aunt Polly and Uncle Alfred Evans, at last with someone who would love me as any child deserves to be loved and not to be treated as something that is always in the way. Just a thought, this was the first time I had been on a bus journey ever, from the station to Killamarsh.

And that dear reader is the tale of how I arrived in the village I love, and the village is KILLAMARSH.

Aunt Polly with my sister Lily.

2. Killamarsh in the 1930s

My most vivid picture of Killamarsh in the 30s has to be the slow pace of living. The horse and cart had not yet passed into history, the lamplighter still cycled round the village to light all the gas lamps in the streets, and the pikelet man toured the village on his tricycle with his basket of wares on the front. To alert the customers he would ring his handbell. How he kept his white clothes so clean was and remains a mystery, considering the state of some of the roads. At this time many of the minor roads were unpaved and the ruts would be filled in with ashes from the residents' fires. We also had a visit from the ice cream man, but only once a week on Sunday afternoons.

The village itself consisted of four Thorpes. By using the word Thorpe, which is of Viking origin, I am not implying that the Vikings had been in the area but who can say? Westthorpe, Upperthorpe, Netherthorpe and the final one was Kirkthorpe, or Churchtown as we know it today. These Thorpes were all connected by roads, some not in very good repair. They were joined by a myriad of footpaths, some of which are still in use today, and they were separated by beautiful green fields which were first class for energetic children to play in.

Then of course, there was the canal. It was closed to barges due to the tunnel cave-in which had occurred in the early 1900s, so in the 1930s it was only used for recreational boating and fishing. But even the boating was fading into the history books due to neglect of the canal.

The first large housing project got under way in the 30s, built to the rear of houses on Rotherham Road on the right hand side as you pass down the road towards Norwood Colliery and the Parish of Wales. It was built to house people moved from condemned housing from the Brickyard just above the canal at Churchtown, families from stone houses in Nethermoor Lane, and more from stone cottages on Barbers Lane.

Rotherham Road

High Moor

Here are some names that may jog a few memories: Watson, Barber, Glossop, Binney, Draper, Webster, Ethel Barker, Bingham, Wheelhouse. The list goes on and on, and I am sure you, the reader, can add many more.

The village itself had a good many shops spread the length and breadth of the settlement, selling a wide range of goods including the boy's favourite sweet, 'gobstoppers'. These were huge, not much smaller than a golfball and would last for hours if you just sucked them. At school it was advisable to have a piece of paper to wrap the sweet up when classes started, then one could resume sucking it at playtime. Whilst in class it was forbidden to eat sweets of any kind.

But the main shopping area was Bridge Street. Churchtown had a row of shops on the righthand side when leaving the church: Keeton's beer-off, a haberdashery shop selling a myriad of goods, Smith's hardware shop selling many other articles, for instance wireless batteries and accumulators. These were essential to power up the wireless sets of the day as they could not be coupled to the electricity circuit that was coming in the near future. There was even a slaughterhouse very nearly opposite the church gates. How's that for planning?

Bridge Street looking north.
Note the petrol pump on the left near the car.
(Photograph courtesy of Vincent Hopkinson)

As well as St Giles Church there were three chapels to cater for Nonconformists. Killamarsh had nine public houses and one club, the Miners' Welfare on Kirkcroft Lane. There was also a very popular cinema which stood where the new doctors' surgery is located. In those days the village had two doctors. Dr Lipp's surgery was in Bridge Street and Dr Murray's surgery was at the junction of Kirkcroft Lane and High Street. A dentist by the name of Reed had a surgery on Sheffield Road.

That was the village as I remember it as a young boy.

3. What we got up to as children

At first I found it hard to bond and make friends, eventually though, I made many pals both boys and dare I say it girls as well. After these initial problems it proved to be plain-sailing.

The first adventure was my first visit to the village cinema, on what was known as 'The Saturday morning Penny-Rush', designed for children only.

This was the first time I had been inside a cinema, (care homes did not cater for these luxuries) and I might add I had the most terrifying hour and a half of my young life. Why you may well ask? I had never heard gunfire, or ever seen Indians shooting arrows into people, men and women alike.

So it was, I spent the rest of the programme with my hands over my eyes. The friend who brought me, Wilfred Evans (no relation to Aunt Polly and Uncle Alfred Evans) wanted to take me home but I stuck it out to the bitter end. I was relieved to get out into the fresh air, where Wilfred finally convinced me after a lot of talking that it was all make believe.

The annual village fair, known as Killamarsh Feast, was held on the first weekend in September. I can only dimly remember the first I went to and it was held opposite the Nags Head pub on a play area near the junction of Westthorpe Road. The fair that I do remember was a travelling fair owned by Messrs. Harness and was held on the land to the rear of the cinema, now occupied by the pre-fabs. The one thing that sticks in my mind from that fair was the taste of the delicious pie and peas, there has not been the like since.

On the Sunday the church of St Giles would hold a service in the afternoon on the fairground and Reverend Milner would use the Noah's Ark as his pulpit. The Noah's Ark was a roundabout where the passengers sat on model animals instead of the usual seats. I attended chapel but this was one church ceremony I was allowed to attend.

On the subject of chapel, I attended Kirkcroft Lane Chapel and every Whitsuntide the chapel would hold what was known as the Chapel Sermons. On this Sunday most of the children wore their new clothes, it was then a custom that new clothes were purchased for the occasion. It should be stressed that not all children received a full outfit, it all hinged on what the parents could afford. Regardless of this no one was sneered at or belittled as money was hard to come by for many of the villagers, anyway they all preened themselves on their way to chapel.

A star card was carried by every child attending chapel which was stamped with a star for each attendance. At the Chapel Sermons a prize would be awarded in the form of a book or similar for good attendance.

The ladies of the chapel choir would sing themselves hoarse, in full flow I thought they were brilliant. Then to finish the service off they would sing that beautiful hymn 'The Day Thou Gavest Lord is Ended', to me this rounded off a very special day in the life of a young boy.

Another major event of the year was the Summer Carnival. The Carnival Queen and her attendants were chosen before the big event and on the day the whole entourage, which included Boy Scouts, Girl Guides, Boys' Brigade, our only policeman to keep law and order and of course Killamarsh Prize Band in the lead would parade through the village. Anyone could join in the parade as it passed through the village, but of course Her Highness and her attendants would be the only ones allowed to ride on a decorated float loaned by a local farmer. The location of the starting point was altered every year, say the West-end pub, the year after, Norwood Colliery then it would be the turn of Station Road next, High-moor the year after. The finishing point was always the Miners Welfare on Kirkcroft Lane. Sadly it is not held anymore. The Queen reigned for a year and was expected to attend any civic functions in the village.

Killamarsh carnival moving down Lock Hill.

This may be the best time to talk about the mischief we got up to and I was just as bad or good as any others I played with.

One amusing trick we played, well amusing to us anyway, we would obtain some rope and tie two adjacent door handles together, knock on both doors at the same time then stand back and watch the fun as both tenants tried to open their doors. Mind you it did not always work, some tenants used their back doors and walked round to the front.

Another trick consisted of a large button, a length of cotton and a drawing pin. The button would be tied to the cotton, the drawing pin was pressed into the wooden window frame, the cotton was passed over the pin, and then from a place of concealment we repeatedly pulled on the cotton to make the button tap on the glass. Of course we had to be prepared to lose everything if we were discovered and had to run away.

On dark nights we would stuff newspaper up cast-iron drainpipes and light the paper, it made a terrifying roaring sound as the flames were drawn up the pipe by the draught, we called it 'The Bull's Roar'.

We would change peoples garden ornaments round, a stone sundial for a stone bird bath and so on.

There were times we were caught and got a clip round the ear for our troubles from the people we had played the trick on. But we never told our parents, because without doubt we would have received more punishment; for instance being kept in, which would never do.

I think at this time I should comment on no less a personage than our local police officer, by the only name I knew him by and that is Bobby Dobbs. What can be said about this man? My one wish is that he could be on the streets today, he would certainly instill some sort of respect in the children of today. When he wore his helmet he looked about eight feet tall which to young people was very intimidating to say the least.

Bobby Dobbs outside his house in School Lane, now Sheffield Road.

In fact when my friends were out on any pretext and we spotted Bobby Dobbs we would automatically cross the street and study whether we had crossed the line recently, did scrumping apples come under that category? He lived halfway down School Lane now called Sheffield Road above the Junior School so mischief in that road was a definite no no. I would not wish the reader to think that this was all we did as boys. We still had our education to attend to, Mr Blaidon saw to that. He was the headmaster of Killamarsh Junior School. I am sorry to admit it but I was not the happiest of pupils. I struggled terribly with maths and science, but enjoyed English, history and woodworking.

My blackest days were always if I was required to write anything. You see, I knew what was coming; being left-handed in those days was almost as bad as having leprosy, or so it seemed to me. It led to having sore and red knuckles after being rapped over them by the teacher. This treatment resulted in my so-called black days, these were the times that I would ask myself, why don't I have a mum and dad like most of my pals, feeling sorry for myself, but it all disappeared when a knock came on the door and a voice saying "Can your Bernard come out to play?" and I was back with my friends once more.

Spintshill Lane

Mansfield Road

Here are some things we did, but not with mischief in mind.

Winter-warmers

A lump of clay was fashioned into a box with no lid. The size was optional but about 4 inches by 2 inches, with 2 inch walls, would be big enough. A hole would be opened in each wall with a pencil, for draught. In the process a wire handle was fitted, similar to a handbag handle, to enable us to carry it when lit. The box then had to be baked in our long-suffering parent's or guardian's oven. Once hard it was filled with touch-wood, which was obtained from a well rotted tree, it was soft to the touch, and did not flame but smouldered and glowed red. Anyone who knew of a source of touch-wood would be the hero of the week. Then we could warm our hands whenever we needed to

Bows and arrows

Being close to the woods at Norwood, we had access to a ready supply of poles for our bows, and in the wood bottom a goodly supply of hazel sticks for the arrows. But these very efficient bows and arrows were used for target practice only and nothing else; to shoot at animals or people was clearly not allowed and anyone who contravened this rule would not be tolerated in the group.

Kites

We would obtain two thin sticks one shorter than the other, and tie them in the form of a cross. All four ends of the cross were linked together with string, this frame was then covered with brown paper. A tail was tied to the long end of the kite to steady it in flight, and what was needed then was yards and yards of thin string, the more string the higher the kite flew.

Model making

This was in great favour, as we could let our imagination run to what ever we chose: ships, tanks and planes, in fact anything appertaining to the war. My favourites were planes: Spitfires, Hurricanes, and after the invasion of France, the Typhoon (also known as the tank buster), all done with a penknife. All these models were made of wood. We preferred boxwood but we not too choosy in this. All self-respecting boys carried a penknife to cut sticks etc. for our bows and arrows and for modelling, but nothing, I repeat nothing unlawful crossed our minds.

Girls played rounders, hopscotch and skipping, the boys preferred whip and top, marbles and of course street football.

A game both sexes could play was called Snobs (no do not ask about the name). Five coloured clay cubes, about the size of Oxo cubes, were held in the cupped hand. A clay marble was placed on the floor, the player then tossed the cubes into the air not too high or they would separate. At the same time, using the same hand, a grab was made to pick up the marble. The player would then try to catch as many cubes on the back of the hand as possible, the number and colours counted as points but if you failed to pick up the marble your score would be nil.

Another game we played was a variant of hide and seek by the name of Kick-Can. It went as follows: one searcher was chosen and the rest of the party would elect one of the group to kick a tin can as far as he or she could, then they would scatter and hide. The searcher had to retrieve the can and place it in its original position before he could commence searching. The cruel twist to the game was that whilst he or she was searching a hider could dash out and kick the can away again, thus causing the searcher to find the can and place it in its original position before he could resume hunting. When a hider was caught he or she would join in the search with the other and so on. What fun we had.

At Christmas came carol singing. At least we could walk the streets without fear of being mugged or worse. The thing that gave us a hard time was the fact that if we did not sing all the verses of the carol it would be pointless knocking on the door for a reward. A carol was a full carol those days, not just one verse. During the war when the blackout was in force we had to know all the carol because we could not use any source of light to read the words.

One year three friends and I were doing our thing in Jubilee Crescent and after visiting two or three houses we knocked on the last one, Mr

Smith our music teacher at school lived there. He asked us in and invited us to sing again, he prompted us on several occasions, and when he seemed satisfied with our performance he sent us on our way with a shilling which was a princely sum those days.

Christmas Eve and New Year's Eve were reserved for going round the local public houses to relate the old Derbyshire saga of 'Old Tup'. We would also visit people's homes and maybe get an invitation to come in and recite it. At the end in all probability we would be given mince pies and a sip of sherry, we may have been a little tipsy after all this. For us the most money would be made at the pubs, but we never did find out whether it was our performance or the effects of alcohol on the listeners.

4. Relating to 'Owd Tup'

One of the highlights of childhood Christmases and New Years was 'gooin rahnd wi towd Tup', though as children we little thought, or cared for that matter, that we were helping to perpetuate a Derbyshire tradition that had its origins back in the days of the Mummers. Our main concern, apart from being allowed to stay out after dark, was the financial aspect.

Weeks were spent in preparation, glory-holes were ransacked and jumble-sales were searched for the requisite clothing: a top-hat or bowler maybe two or more sizes too big, for the Mester; a dress, bonnet and boned corsets for Sally, the corsets were worn on the outside of the dress and, of course, an apron for the butcher.

The Tup's head was the item on which we lavished the most attention. Usually two old brush heads fastened together, the bristles forming the teeth and the bottom brush sawn in two and hinged for the bottom jaw. The tongue would be at least a foot long and made from an old red bicycle inner tube and the eyes were the biggest marbles we could find. The marbles we preferred were made of glass and reflected the light and being multi-coloured appeared more lifelike, they were called 'Ponty marbles'. Cow horns and sheep's wool gleaned from barbed wire fencing of the sheep fields completed the effigy.

Then nostrils were burned right through the head with a red hot poker and lengths of gas tubing were fitted to the back of the holes. The boy playing the Tup could then light a fag-end as he crouched under the blanket forming the body and, in between coughs, make the Tup emit smoke in the most theatrical manner. Inevitably, during the course of the evening he would set either his hair, clothing or the blanket alight, but it all added to the entertainment.

When the big night came we would blacken our faces, dress up in our respective togs and with a Kale knife for the butcher, a goodly supply of fag-ends for the Tup (collected from the pavements on dry days) and of course, the collecting tin, we would set off. For the curious a Kale knife was used by farmers, it had to be large and sharp to cut the woody stalks of the kale, in fact it could be likened to a modern day machete. However, our parents blunted the blade to avoid accidents to us 'actors'.

Judging the exact time to start was crucial, too early and we got nowt, too late and someone else had already been. Knocking on the first door, we would chant the preamble as loudly as we could, sometimes we were told to remove ourselves, but mostly we were encouraged to perform on the doorstep or in the house.

An invitation to come in usually meant not only a larger contribution but also a mince pie and a drink, and there were always those who pressed us to have a drink knowing that as the evening wore on our performances would reflect our increasing state of intoxication. Best of all from the financial point of view was too be allowed inside a pub, club or dancehall if we were lucky.

Nowadays, apart from sporadic attempts to revive the custom, the Old Tup is no longer a feature of the Christmas or New Year scene at least not in the part of Derbyshire where I live.

In these days of sophisticated entertainment there seems to be no room for such simple and repetitive performances, except, maybe in the hearts of us who mourn the passing of the reminders of our youth, and who will always join in the refrain 'Poor owd Tup, Poor owd Tup'

To understand what occurred to OWD TUP, please read on.

5. More of 'Owd Tup'

RECITE:

Mester: Here comes me and ahr owd lass, short o' money and short o' brass.

All SING:

We have a little tup sir, comes knocking at your door.

And if you let us in sir, we'll please you more and more.

Poor owd tup, Poor owd tup.

ENTER AND SING.

As I was going to market, on a market day,

I saw the finest tup sir that ever fed on hay.

Poor owd tup, Poor owd tup.

DIALOGUE:

Mester: Sally, Sally is there a butcher in this tahn?

Sally: Ah, mi Uncle Bob's a blacksmith.

Mester: We want a Butcher not a Blacksmith, yer silly block-eed!

Butcher: Here I am, a jolly butcher. What's to be done?

Mester: Kill this tup.

Butcher: Wheer shall I stick him?

Mester: As tha been a butcher all these years and tha dont know where ter stick a tup?

Butcher: Ah can cut four pahnd er beef off a bare leg o' mutton. Nah, where shall I stick him?

In the heart sir or in the rump sir?

Put thi hand o'er his eyes.

(Sally puts her hand on the rear of tup)

Butcher: Them's not his eyes you silly beggar, put thi hands o'er his eyes.

Sally does so and the butcher stabs tup, tup bleats, threshes about and dies noisily.

ALL SING

The butcher has killed the tup sir, in danger of his life,

He's up to his knees in blood sir and wants a longer knife.

Poor owd tup, Poor owd tup.

The horns grew on the tup sir, they grew so mighty high,

That every time he nods his head, they scrape the bright-blue sky.

Poor owd tup, Poor owd tup.

The wool that grew on tup sir, grew so mighty high,

The ravens built their nest in it; I heard their young ones cry.

Poor owd tup, Poor owd tup.

All the lads in Derby came begging for his eyes,

To kick up and down the streets cos they were football size.

Poor owd tup, Poor owd tup.

All the women in Derby came begging for his ears,

To make them leather aprons to last 'em forty years,

Poor owd tup, Poor owd tup.

All the men in Derby came begging for his tail,

To ring St George's passing bell that hung in Derby jail.

Poor owd tup, Poor owd tup.

And now ahr song is ended, we have no more to say,

So please to give us a Christmas box, and let us on our way,

POOR OWD TUP – POOR OWD TUP.

Acknowledgements to Dave Froggat for preserving this, and other parts of our history.

6. Chores and jobs

Being a juvenile in the 30s and 40s did not consist of nothing but playtime, my friends and I had responsibilities regarding chores around the home. For instance I was expected to ensure that the coal buckets were kept full at all times with the exception of school hours. Another task was to chop wood for kindling, and running errands to the local shops when required.

On Monday mornings my first job was to light the fire under the big copper so hot water in large quantities was available for wash-day (a job I enjoyed, what boy does not like lighting fires?). A copper was a large cast iron vessel capable of holding at least 10 gallons of water, set in a brick surround with the fireplace underneath, complete with chimney. The water would be heated to boiling point and would be topped up through the day as the hot water was used in the washing cycle.

If I was not at school, during the holidays, I was needed to turn the mangle (no one had spin-driers in the 30s and 40s). To me the mangle seemed to be a gigantic, clanking machine with massive wooden rollers which looked quite capable of swallowing my aunt as well as the clothes it was squeezing as much moisture as it possibly could from. You see my aunt was not as tall as the mangle and, as her hands got closer to the rollers, I would slow down so much I would receive a scolding with the inference that wash-day was long enough without a go-slow operating the instrument. What I did not realize was that my aunt was more in tune with the mangle and knew how near to get to the rollers with her hands.

My favourite chore was for an old lady by the name of Mrs Silvers who lived further down Norwood Lane. She and I had an agreement which was as follows: if I ran all her errands for a week she would reward me with, no not money, but with a comic-book with the name of 'The Wizard'. It was more a reader's comic than page after page of pictures, it contained stories which were serialized week after week.

The Wizard was a veritable mine of adventure stories which in my opinion could not be bettered today. One such saga is still fresh in my mind, it was called The Wolf of Kabul and centered round the exploits of an Englishman and his Tibetan side-kick by the name of Chung whose only weapon was a battered old cricket bat which was held together by binding it with copper wire. I know today it may sound ridiculous but Chung called this fearsome weapon 'Clickey bar'. One has to assume that was as near to English as he could get, nevertheless, however silly it may sound, that story transported me to Afghanistan and to most of the Asian continent week in week out, happy days and well worth the errands.

Also can any reader remember Desperate Dan and his famous Cow-pies with the cow's horns sticking out of the pie-crust?

One of the more onerous jobs I had to do included taking a bucket and shovel to collect horse droppings, which I might add were very plentiful those days. My uncle would use these to fertilize his garden. I also visited fields in which sheep were grazing, to collect their droppings which my uncle used for his cucumbers. I think I should explain the sheep-droppings in a little more detail. My Uncle Alf would place the droppings into a bucket or similar container and cover them with water. After a few days maturing, he would take a woollen sock, placing one end in the liquid and the other end buried at the roots of the cucumber plant. Capillary action ensured that the plant received the right amount of fertilizer it needed. Result, some fantastic 'cumbers' as he would call them.

These chores gave us boys and girls a sense of responsibility which would in most cases carry on into our adult lives. My belief is that children should be given the chance to do small tasks on a regular basis to help them mature into well rounded citizens, forgive me if you think I am preaching, but it is a subject I feel strongly about.

Before I go any further I feel I should talk about how my idyllic boyhood suffered a violent jolt and if I am to be true to my story I am obliged to relate what occurred.

Nothing runs as smoothly as one would desire and another severe hiccup happened in my boyhood when I reached about twelve and a half years of age. My errant father and stepmother decided, probably as I was approaching school leaving age, that they should have the benefit of my working life. So one day they came to Aunt Polly's and demanded that they should have me back and stated that they would call in the lawyers if Aunt Polly did not comply with their demands. I was at school and Uncle Alf was at work at Kiveton Colliery so Aunt Polly was on her own to face these people and as I was not adopted she thought she had no alternative but to let me go. When I arrived home from school my belongings were packed and so began another chapter.

I started at Edlington school and hated every minute of it, I had no friends there and as I pointed out earlier I was so withdrawn I found it almost impossible to bond with anyone. My new guardians had already taken my brother Leslie away from my sister Edith and he was employed at Yorkshire Main Colliery Edlington. This meant I had no brother to help as I was the victim of a quite considerable amount of bullying.

But the worst thing I had to deal with was my life at number 2 Staveley Street, Edlington which went as follows: when I got up every (and I must emphasize 'every' morning) before going to school I had to prepare all the vegetables required for dinner that day, whether it be potatoes, cabbage, carrots or cauliflower when in season. After school I was obliged to wash up all the crockery and pans, then stepmother had me take 'her' dog for a walk for at least 30 minutes. I know it is wrong but I hated that dog nearly as much as the owner.

This is the period I take no pride in whatsoever, in fact it brings shame on me to relate it, but to be true to my story it must be put on record. I think it is fair to say that Leslie and I were on the slippery slope to end up as criminals at this time as both of us had been involved in shoplifting. Luckily we were not caught. But the incident I recall that stopped us in our tracks went as follows: I make no excuses, but we were hungry and anyone who has been hungry will understand what I mean. Leslie and I and a boy called Geoff walked into the Maypole grocery store in Edlington. Geoff went right into the store, Leslie and I stood just inside the door, to the rear of us were shelves stacked with tea-cakes, these were sweet bread cakes laced with currants or sultanas.

As Geoff passed us on his way out Leslie and I grabbed several tea-cakes each. As we turned to leave the store the manager saw what we were up to and shouted "Put those back and stay where you are". We were terrified so we took the only option open to us, both of us stopped and threw the teacakes at the manager to confuse him long enough so we could make our escape. I am pleased to say we succeeded in doing that.

Now comes the unbelievable bit. Geoff had been able to stroll away from the store, and when we caught up with him a little later he opened his raincoat and displayed an 18 inch slab of Genoa fruit cake. How he got that slab of cake into his coat remains a mystery to me even to this day.

The occurrence that brought the seriousness of what we had done came on the Monday morning when the store manager came to school with a police officer to try to identify the boys who were guilty of this crime. Thankfully he failed to identify any one of us. After this we needed no prompting to stay on the straight and narrow, and anyway I did not stay in the situation much longer that produced such behaviour.

I carried on for nearly a year. Then one day Leslie and I both came home together and we found to our horror that the roller skates and air gun given to us by the colliery manager's son were missing from where we kept them. We asked our stepmother if she knew where they were and she calmly told us that the person we had to call Father had sold them to one of her friends. I especially was heartbroken as the skates were top class, they had had ball-bearing wheels and rubber cushioning underneath at each end of the skate. And I had learned to skate whilst taking that dog of hers a walk. Leslie, who was only too aware of how we were being treated, said one Friday, if he gave me the money for bus fare would I think about running away to my sister Doris in Sheffield? I was terrified at the prospect of what would happen when they discovered that I had gone but nevertheless I said yes, I would go.

So on the following Friday Leslie gave me some money for the bus fare from Doncaster to Sheffield. I would have to walk to Balby near Doncaster as the bus went through there on its way to Sheffield via Conisbrough. The money he gave me was part of his spending money, that was the reason for the walk. This was a very brave and unselfish act on Leslie's part as he did not know what the repercussions would be, and I honour him for it.

So on the following Monday I set off for school as usual, and then set off on what I thought was the greatest test of my young life. It has to be remembered that the only thing I could take with me was my gas-mask in its Oster-milk tin, and what I stood up in which was shirt, jumper, trousers, knee stockings and canvas shoes and no coat. This is how I arrived at sister Doris's. She was very hard up as her husband was in the forces and she could not work as she suffered with lung problems as did many others who lived in this heavily industrialised city. Doris did her best for a while in this very trying situation then she said she had reached her limit and suggested that I visit my Aunt Polly and Uncle Alf for a while to ease some of the pressure on her. Needless to say I jumped at the chance to see my Square Lady and Uncle again.

I caught the Beauchief company coach which plied between Sheffield and Worksop stopping at the Travellers Rest at Highmoor in Killamarsh. When I left the bus I wished I had wings on my heels such was my need to see them again at 44 Rotherham Road. I could not get there fast enough. When I walked in my aunt burst into tears, as did I, and when Uncle Alf arrived from work at 2.30pm the first thing he said was that there was no way would I have to go back to those people.

He then instructed my aunt to apply for a new ration book, at the same time he told her to take me to the shops and get me some clothes and shoes using their clothing coupons, and then enrol me at school.

Father and stepmother finally found out my whereabouts and made an attempt to get me back but failed. Uncle Alf, all 6ft 2inches of him, advised my so-called father not to put a foot through his front gate unless he was tired of living or words to that effect. I was home again with my real parents and friends never to leave Killamarsh again, not under those circumstances anyway.

7. Billy Whewell Fishmonger

Allow me to introduce a little levity to this story. Does anyone remember Billy Whewell our local fishmonger, selling not only fish but rabbits as well? The problem was, he kept the rabbits covered up, arousing people's suspicions, thinking they had been caught illegally by poachers.

I lived in Rotherham Road and on the opposite side of the road lived a family by the name of Bennet, and they were the proud possessors of a beautiful and talkative parrot. Billy Whewell always parked his cart outside Bennets to ply his trade. Whilst serving his customers we and nearly all of Rotherham Road would hear the parrot screeching over and over again "does your mother want a rabbit?" intermixed with some choice Anglo-Saxon words, at which point Billy would say to Mrs. Bennet: "if tha dunt shut that b----y bird up I will wring it's b----y neck and anyone else's who tries to stop me". The amusing thing about this was, that he was about as far through as one of his kippers, by that remark I mean he was extremely thin and puny.

The only thing that would shut the bird up would be when Billy moved to another pitch.

There was a childrens rhyme doing the rounds at the time which went like this: "Billy Whewell sells fish three ha-pence a dish don't buy it don't buy it it stinks when you fry it". Many are the times that my friends and I have had to make a hasty retreat after giving our rendering of it.

8 Making pegged rugs

O n winter nights when the weather prevented me from going out, I recall sitting at a small table cutting strips of cloth 1 inch wide and 3 inches long, to enable my aunt and uncle to use them in the process of making pegged rugs, another name for them was Hearth Rugs.

It has to be said that some beautiful rugs were created not only by my guardians but most working class families. As money was in short supply, not many miners and other workers could afford to carpet their homes, as is the trend today. So, with that in mind an explanation into this work is needed as this and many other things are no longer done in the home.

My aunt would be obliged to obtain a sugar sack from the local grocer, these sacks were used because they were more closely woven than the hessian sacks, having said that, sometimes hessian had to be utilized if nothing else was available.

My uncle would open up the sack by cutting down the seam and if they planned on a large rug two sacks would be sewn together. Then came the material, it had to be woven cloth, knitted garments could not be used because the knitted piece would tend to unravel; so old coats, trousers, dresses in fact any old items of clothing that were closely woven were acceptable with the exception of underwear.

If a design was decided upon it was first drawn onto the sacking, for instance if a diamond in the centre was planned then the outline would be followed in tufts of the colour decided upon, then the diamond would be filled in with that shade. If a butterfly or flower design was planned and was formed in a multi-colored pattern, then every colour change would be edged and then filled in by that colour until the complete flower or butterfly appeared.

How was this achieved? With a broken clothes peg with one leg remaining, this leg was sharpened to a point. I remember my guardians having a spat over who was using their peg, one would think they were personalised. The purpose of the peg was to pierce the sacking, then one end of the strip of material would be pushed through the sacking and pulled half-way through then it would be doubled back and threaded into a new hole as close as possible to the first thus forming a U shape through the sacking. Now comes the clever bit, each tuft had to be placed as close as possible to its neighbour so that each one was held upright by the one next to it, too far apart would result in the tufts flopping over (disaster!).

After the design was outlined the background would be filled in, with the exception of a two-inch border all the way round the rug. This was turned under and sewn into place to prevent the sacking from fraying.

If these rugs were made properly they would last for years, and in my eyes they were works of art, most of the ladies of the 30s and 40s were veritable artists due to having the knowledge passed on by former generations. I hope this explains how these rugs were made, I could possibly show you better than writing about it.

9. Killamarsh during the war

I was fast approaching my eleventh birthday, and the war clouds that had settled over Europe were now spreading across the English Channel to cover the whole of the British Isles.

Adolf Hitler had taken Austria and also marched into the Sudetenland, which he believed was German due to many of the people speaking the the German language. However this section was part of the country of Czechoslovakia, which he then proceeded to march into. It has been said many times that Britain and France betrayed Czechoslovakia by believing Hitler when he stated that after Sudetenland he held no more territorial ambitions.

Hitler, thinking with the support of Russia he could get away with it again, then ordered his troops into the little country of Poland. Britain and France stood firm and told him that if he did not pull his troops out of Poland a state of war would be declared.

I well remember that morning, at 11am September the 3rd 1939 the Prime Minister Neville Chamberlain informed all the people listening to the radio that Hitler had not done what they required, and ended with these chilling words, "and consequently this country is at war with Germany".

And so it began, Britain had to become a fortress as soon as possible, our troops were sent to France to help if that country was attacked. As a country we had a lot of catching up to do as we were not ready for war. The so-called 'phoney war', which meant that not much was happening, gave us some breathing space, so we were able to build air-raid shelters and boost our production of all types of arms, including fighter planes. Then came the Battle of France, then Dunkirk and the Battle of Britain, I have passed over this pretty quickly so I can describe how this was affecting Killamarsh, with no thought at all of belittling what our Army, Navy and Air Force were going through.

In the village, to boost the production of munitions, all iron railings were taken and more or less anything metallic was accepted, so the ladies co-operated by giving up their alloy saucepans. Whether they were used for that purpose has been debated ever since.

The lamplighter ceased lighting the street lights, the pikelet seller was ordered to stop ringing his handbell, the reason being, a handbell would be rung if poison gas had been dropped in the vicinity. Double-summertime, this means we were 2 hours in advance of Greenwich mean time, was introduced presumably to lengthen the working day so more work could be done. It has been said work on the farms would continue until eleven at night, especially at harvest time.

As the fear of a German invasion grew all road signs were removed to confuse the invaders if the worst did happen. Tank-traps, consisting of railway lines concreted into the road, were set at the top of Lock Hill with about five feet protruding out of the ground. And of course all young men not in essential work were conscripted into the forces. This caused gaps in families, some alas which were never to be filled again.

Air raid wardens patrolled the streets at night and if you were showing one glimmer of light through your blackout curtains you could be heavily fined. The familiar cry at that time was, "Put that b----y light out," whether there was an air-raid on or not. To protect the children of the southern cities from bombing they were evacuated to the countryside. Killamarsh billeted a number of them, and I for one wondered what torment some of them were going through. By the same token a number took to it like ducks to water and enjoyed the situation they were in, because some of them had never seen green fields, cows eating grass, and some did not even know where milk came from.

In the Great War 1914-1918, as you well know, the Germans used poison gas, and so the government said that everyone should be supplied with a gas mask. Tiny babies had one that completely enclosed them. After placing the baby inside, the container would be sealed and to enable the baby to breathe, a crude air-pump was fitted to be operated by an adult. When the baby was enclosed in this thing it was terrified, and indeed some of the mothers were even more upset than their offspring some even saying they would never use them. Thankfully it never came to that.

Your gas mask had to be with you at all times even in the loo. We were also obliged to carry identity cards, my number was RCSA 2743. No infringement of human rights those days, only Adolf Hitler did things like that.

Once the Germans started to bomb the cities the authorities closed all places of entertainment including theatres and cinemas, with the exception of public houses. But they were forced to rescind this order after a very short time, due to public pressure.

At the same time all schools were closed until further notice (Hurray), but again it was only for a short time (Boo) until the windows and doors were treated with strips of sticky paper applied in a diamond pattern to counteract the effects of bomb blast on glass. The school then opened for two hours in the morning to hand out homework to be collected by the pupils to be completed at home and then brought back the following morning, when more would be collected. This went on for a while and then the schools opened full time once more (Woe was me).

If there had been an air raid warning or air raid during the previous night we would have our normal school work in the morning and then in the afternoon session we would be given the choice either to go to sleep or read a book. I always chose a book as I loved reading and still do.

Parents were encouraged to join the air raid wardens, fire watchers, or join the LDV whose full title was Land Defence Volunteers, shortly to become the Home Guard. These men were formed to assist the regular troops in the event of the Germans coming.

I must tell you this story, but make no mistake I am not making fun of, and do not intend to be insulting to anyone in Killamarsh Home Guard. As I told you earlier I attended the chapel on Kirkcroft Lane and after the service I walked home along Kirkcroft Lane towards Bridge Street. I espied a group of Home Guard in the middle of an exercise. They had been ordered to cross the bridge unseen, and as there was a heavy electric cable fastened to the bridge wall they decided to walk along this cable while holding on to the bridge parapet with their hands. As the six or seventh man stood on the cable the supports gave way and all the men on the cable fell into the canal. Luckily the water was not very deep or there could have been a tragedy, instead it turned out to be hilarious, even today it still amuses me when I think of it.

Food rationing was introduced so we children were asked to help supplement the rations by going to the woods at Woodall Ponds where in the past birds had deposited raspberry seeds, by one way or another take your pick, and the raspberry canes had grown in their thousands. We boys and (girls under duress I hasten to add) would fill jars, tins and boxes with these delicious fruits which were free to whoever wanted them.

Parents would use them to make pies, jams and raspberry vinegar which was scrumptious on pancakes, or it could be used as a medicine for anyone who was suffering from a heavy cold or sore throat.

Blackberry picking was a task we enjoyed because we anticipated the delicious blackberry and apple pies that would be forthcoming (and if any reader has not eaten one of these pies all I can say is, you have not lived). To us children this was epitomy of luxury. Bramble jelly could also be made if sugar could be spared.

On lovely misty autumnal mornings, I would walk to the fields on the tunnel top, above the canal tunnel where the mushrooms seemed to appear as if by magic, and in my opinion were more tasty than the ones mass-produced today. My Uncle Alf was employed at Kiveton Colliery and would cycle to and from work. On his way through the fields he would espy mushys as he called them, some of them could be as large as tea-plates, he would not have been able see the small ones whilst riding his cycle. How we enjoyed our breakfasts!

Again in the autumn we visited the wood bottoms via Charlie Walker's farm to collect hazel nuts, which if stored properly could be eaten at Christmas. The trick was to store them somewhere cool and slightly damp, and then the kernels would not dry out, really if you think about it that is what squirrels do.

Another autumn project was collecting horse chestnuts or conkers. We would go to Barlborough Park, which had the best nut bearing trees in the area. Our big problem was that the local boys had already been, and using pieces of wood to throw and knock the nuts down also causing damage to the trees. The legacy of this was, when we visited the park we were chased off by the park-keeper. But with a little patience and waiting a little longer the trees themselves would give up their fruits. We always returned and in the end we obtained the nuts we required, which reminds me of the bruised knuckles sustained playing conkers.

I should now move to November, this was the time that eating chestnuts were ripe and ready for gathering. These nuts were not as prolific in the immediate area as conkers were. The main venue was a small village called Cuckney situated on the border of Nottinghamshire, and the only way we could get there at this time was by cycle. By the way as I said earlier the war was raging and the woods where the nuts were doubled as an Army camp and munitions store and as such was manned by regular troops.

So in theory we were not allowed in the woods or anywhere near, but the soldiers allowed us to gather the nuts as long as we kept well away from the stored bombs, shells and other munitions. When we arrived home after these expeditions we would be welcomed by the children who were either too young or were not fortunate enough to own a cycle. At times we gave so many away it meant we had to make several trips whilst the nuts were plentiful.

And I can tell you readers now there is nothing to match sitting in front of a blazing coal fire roasting self-gathered chestnuts on the prongs of a wire toasting fork, with your family around you.

During the war no bonfires or fireworks were allowed due to blackout regulations, which meant that we children could not perpetuate the story of Guy Fawkes and his unfortunate end. So when the war finally ended the children, no not me I was too old for these childish things, or so I thought, were able to enjoy all the things associated with Guy Fawkes night: fireworks, burning the Guy, roast potatoes, sausages on sticks and pie and peas.

But I am a little in front of myself, we must backtrack at least two weeks before bonfire night. We as teenagers would comb the houses and shops for kindling to burn on the big night. If the above sources could not come up with the goods we were forced to adopt other ways to obtain firewood, so the rascals of Norwood whom I will write about later would visit Highmoor bonfire site and 'borrow' as much wood as we could handle to boost the size of our fire. The kids of Highmoor would be hopping mad at this outrage so they would descend on Churchtown or Nethermoor and take as much wood as they thought they had lost. Then the injured parties from Churchtown and Nethermoor would wait until they thought things had settled down, then guess what, the scheming imps came to Norwood and purloined some of our hard earned wood, I mean to say how cheeky can some people get?

And so it went on, talk about never ending circles. But it all ended peacefully and everyone must have ended up with the same amount of wood they started with. My word the fun we all had, and it gave Guy Fawkes night something we could talk about until the coming of Christmas.

Ah yes, Christmas in those hard up days so long ago! Families those days had very little money to spend on gifts, there were certainly no £200 presents and it was almost unforgivable to go into debt to celebrate the birth of Christ, with the exception of maybe the sixpenny club run by Bramhalls of Bridge Street as my wife remembers.

As stated earlier Christmas was celebrating the birth of Christ, so a number of adults mostly males would let their hair down by having extra drinking hours in the local pubs. At this point think 'Old Tup' for us children and carol singing round the estates as described earlier.

During the war, on the day school broke up for the Christmas holiday the kitchen staff and the teachers would organise parties mainly in the classrooms. All pupils were required to bring to school, a cup, plate and spoon. It was not an elaborate affair, remember the war was still being fought, but we enjoyed sandwiches in all probability they would be potted meat, then we had jelly and a bun, also a cup of tea or orange juice not the real stuff it was artificial but we liked it.

The jelly was made with a substance called gelatin which is tasteless and transparent it is derived from collagen, and is usually purchased in a thin sheet or block form. When boiling water is applied it dissolved, fruit juice and food colourant would be added then the mixture was set aside to cool and set, hey presto a 'delicious war-time jelly.'

After we had tucked into the goodies the pupils and teachers would exchange Christmas cards, and leave the school brimming over with anticipation of what the season would bring to us all.

But Christmas Eve was something special for me. As a very lucky boy I would hang up one of my uncle's pit stockings. These were preferable due to their length, anything else would have been too small. I would hang mine at the end of the mantlepiece, this being the shelf which was fixed over the top of the fireplace which allowed ornaments and maybe a clock, wives would have a wire fixed underneath it to hang small items of washing on (think fire hazard at this point). However, this stocking always ended up hanging on the bed-head the following morning.

Is there anyone that can remember the exquisite smell that pervaded the bedroom on Christmas morning and only then resulting from the scent of the apples and oranges (when available)? My stocking would contain one or both fruits, a book, sometimes an adventure story or an annual such as the Beano or Dandy, or similar; a small toy; one or two new pennies; sweets and a few nuts again, if they were available and that would be it.

One special Christmas I will never forget went something like this: I always slept in the same room as the hot water tank as it was the warmest and it also had a double bed, but I woke on Christmas morning in another bedroom and in a single bed. To my joy and excitement my eldest brother Billy had come home on leave from the Navy, he was serving on submarines.

But sadly this was to be the last time that I would see him. Some months later we received the awful news that he had been lost in the Mediterranean. The submarine had struck a mine and sank with all hands.

There was also the excitement of Christmas dinner with plum-pudding and all the trimmings, the tea party when family and friends gathered to talk of old times and what they thought the future held for us all, (no repeat films those days).

I feel strongly at this point that I should mention an occurrence during my stay at the care home. One Christmas morning I awoke to the sound of brother Leslie playing with his presents however few, and after searching for my gifts for a while and failing to find any I burst into tears thinking I had been passed over. When Nurse Wainwright who was in charge of the home heard this she explained that when Father Christmas had entered our room I had stirred and, thinking I was waking up, he left my presents downstairs. I went down as fast as my legs would take me and there they were on the breakfast table not a lot but to be enjoyed by a happy little boy once more.

Now I am getting soppy so let us change the subject. Daytrips! Before the war started and maybe a few months into the war (the phoney war as it was called), my aunt and uncle would take me on a day trip to the east coast in the summer when and if they could afford it.

Author aged 13 with Aunt Polly and six-year old nephew David

We would get up early that morning, I had not slept very much that night due I suppose to the excitement, so it did not take me long to be ready. With other families we would walk up the fields to Kiveton Station, a distance of about 2 miles, if a bus was not available to meet the train, by road it was just over 3 miles. It seemed to be packed to capacity but we always managed to get on. When one is a child it seems to take years to arrive at the seaside, but when we did arrive the train pulled up right on the seafront. Oh the wonder of building sand castles, collecting shells of long dead animals and seaweed. I remember coming home tired out but laden with my trophies, shells, pebbles and 'seaweed', I had to sneak that home because my aunt said it smelt horrible so I could not resist it. I almost forgot to mention the rock with the word Cleethorpes all the way through it to share with my pals.

During the war we were not allowed on to the beaches under any circumstances, because they had been sown with mines as reception areas for the German invaders.

After the war I enjoyed many trips to Blackpool with my aunt and uncle, but it always seemed to be overflowing with people. What I am trying to say, it was far too busy for my taste. After this the trips I enjoyed most were the visits to the coast with my future wife Margaret. So what if it was only Cleethorpes, it could just as easily have been the Riviera, such was our contentment in each other's company.

10. War comes closer

While we children were continuing with our lives in peaceful Killamarsh the war was still raging and the allies were having set-back after set-back. In the Far East the Japanese had entered the war, and were driving us back towards India; at the same time we were fighting the Germans and Italians in Europe and North Africa, but at last our Russian allies had taken some of the pressure off.

In England the Blitz was taking its toll on the civilian population in London, Southampton, Coventry and other major cities. Scotland also suffered when Glasgow was bombed.

It was inevitable that sooner or later it would be the turn of Sheffield to suffer, and so it was, the German terror tactics were let loose on our city for what seemed to be a life-time. When it was in full spate, we in our shelters would have to listen to the people of Sheffield suffering the terrible pounding the Luftwaffe was handing out.

I had a sister living at number 4 Shortridge Street in Attercliffe and I managed to persuade my Aunt Polly to let me visit my sister during a lull in the bombing as we were getting terrible stories of death and destruction so she reluctantly said yes. On the tram travelling along Attercliffe Common I saw to my horror the row upon row of homes that had been blasted into rubble as a result of the bombing, this from an enemy who said they only bombed military targets and factories.

I was overjoyed to see my sister Doris was unhurt, but appalled to discover later that thousands were either dead or injured. The sight that is still with me after all these years, is that scattered over some of the debris were children's toys and whoever owned them would not be playing with them ever again. It was a sickening thought.

In the coming months or years many heart-rending stories would emerge, but many more would never be heard. For instance I heard of the bomb that hit the Marples Hotel in the centre of Sheffield destroying not only the building but all the people inside in seconds.

During one of these raids a German bomber sustained some damage and the pilot decided to jettison his remaining bombs. One of them fell into what is now known as the Rother Valley Country Park and it lay undiscovered for thirty odd years.

Now even we youngsters began to wonder where it would all end. Would we survive, let alone win during the raids on Sheffield? I mean, how near could it get?

After the disaster of France, Dunkirk, Singapore and North Africa the sinking of our finest battleship HMS Hood, and the loss of the cruisers Rodney and Repulse in the Pacific, at last things started to improve after the Battle of Alamein. The Russians were beginning to hold the German forces and in places even to drive them back, and we were slowly turning things round in the Atlantic. By now we also had America fighting alongside us in all the countries that the Axis powers had invaded.

It was about this time that Hitler sank to a new low, he set about sending unmanned flying bombs which were called V1s, or Doodle Bugs, to cause even more terror on the population of English towns and cities. Once set on course and then launched the Germans had no control over them whatsoever, and when they reached this country the engine would cut out and the weapon would fall to earth and on impact would explode with terrific force.

One Sunday morning I had got up early, maybe I was going fishing, the time was between six and seven o'clock, when my uncle and I heard this strange put-put-put sound, we dashed outside and saw the strangest

Hitler's first vengeance weapon the V1 Flying bomb.
The warhead contained 1,870lb of high explosive. It flew at a maximum
speed of 310 mph and had a range of around 150 miles.
(Photograph courtesy of Emmanuel Eichler www.ww2incolour.com)

looking aircraft flying over our estate going east to west. After passing over us the rocket engine cut out and it crashed just inside Cow Lane on the right hand side with an almighty explosion.

But worse was to befall London and the home counties. The V2 Rocket was even more dangerous because it was not heard until it exploded on impact, the reason being it travelled faster than the speed of sound so there was no way of intercepting it. After the explosion came the terrible whooshing noise as the sound caught up.

11. How We Helped

There were schemes every so often to raise funds for the armed forces, for instance the ladies of the village would hold what they called 'knitting bees'. They knitted balaclava helmets, gloves, socks and scarves for our boys over there. But the schemes I remember were 'Buy a Spitfire' weeks. In aid of this our school, Killamarsh Secondary Modern under the Headmastership of Mr Seston, decided to put on a school show. This was to be held at the Miners' Welfare opposite the chapel on Kirkcroft Lane. My word, what an evening that turned out to be.

There were mini plays based on the war, the school choir sang all the patriotic songs twice over, including The Volga Boatman for our Russian allies. I thought it was a bit overlong, but that was only my opinion as I wanted the next part to commence as soon as possible. This was an exhibition of physical fitness by the boys of the school. The reason for all this fuss? Yes, you have guessed it, I was included in the group. Everyone put their heart and soul into what became the talking point for weeks. I never did find out how much money was raised, but never mind, I had played a part in it.

Then there was potato picking. In late October schoolchildren were encouraged to go to a local farm to help with the harvesting of the potato crop; but we were only allowed to work school hours which were 9.00am to 3.30pm. We were paid wages but we always thought these were not enough considering the back-breaking work involved. We were allowed to take home what were called 'oven-busters', the extra large potatoes that were not saleable. To judge how large they were, two would easily fill a bucket.

Whilst on the subject of farms, my sister Lily was employed by Mr George Leah of Netherhouse Farm as dairy-maid, cook and housekeeper. During my school holidays I would help out on the farm with, of course, George Leah's permission. As an adventurous boy, I would tackle any task given to me. I was allowed to milk certain cows, I say certain because some cows would only allow George Leah or the farmhand George Hardy to get anywhere near them. The bull's residence was out of bounds to me. He was from pedigree stock and as such, was on a very short fuse, in fact on his off days he would tolerate no one near his stall.

George Hardy (left) and George Leah

Netherhouse farm, Killamarsh 1940. (Back row) George Hardy (left), my sister Lily. Kneeling on right, Cyril Lindley with Eric Greaves in front. Others unknown.

My sister would churn cream into butter which was in short supply during the war. Now, you must have an idea of why I so enjoyed my days on the farm. However, we lived fairly well under wartime laws of rationing. There were shortages, but being on a farm one could supplement one's diet with farm produce: butter, eggs and chicken, and every so often George Leah would have a pig butchered. He was obliged by law to report the killing, but strangely the carcass seemed to lose weight while being cut up (hmm).

We are supposed to be raking the hay! Author (left), baby David Lindley and Don Lindley. Unknown boy in the centre.

I suppose my favourite time on the farm had to be the harvest, gathering the wheat, barley and oats. I used to think the threshing machine had magical powers, being able to do all the tasks asked of it, and nothing, but nothing, could match the smell of the steam engine that supplied all the power for the threshing machine by means of belts and pulleys.

There were quite a number of people who would help out at this time and they all knew each other. In fact, harvest could be likened to a family get-together, everyone got on so well, it was a shame it had to end, as did my summer holidays.

There were other activities such as Dig for Victory where the government asked everyone to cultivate every piece of land they could and even I got the bug. My uncle gave me a portion of his garden and told me it was my responsibility to look after it. Surprise, surprise, I found I was enjoying growing things and eating them. I grew lettuce, radishes, spring onions and peas, but (confession time) not many peas saw the inside of a saucepan, but that experience stood me in good stead and I still love gardening as I reach the grand old age of (never mind).

Then came the day I had to put away childish things and buckle down and earn my living and help with the war effort.

My Uncle Alf took me to Ross and Sons on Forge Lane and obtained employment for me there. The factory manufactured magnets for timing mechanisms for large and small bombs. They also made the track chain links for tanks. My uncle said there was no way I was going down the mines.

Before I started work my uncle said I needed a more reliable bike as my job would depend on me getting to work on time. A friend of his at Kiveton informed him he was selling his Carlton racing cycle and he would let me buy it for £7.10 shillings. This to me was a king's ransom, as I had very little saved up. Uncle Alf came up trumps and put the rest of the money with mine and so I became the proud owner of one of the top cycles in production at that time. (I will describe the bike later).

At Ross's I was a general dogsbody for a while, then one of the moulding machine operators was called up to join the forces. Mr Ross asked me if I thought I could do the job and I jumped at the chance. So I became the youngest machine moulder in the factory and, credit where credit is due, Mr Ross paid me adult wages from then on until I myself received my calling up papers for the forces.

Before going on, I take this chance to tell you about a small adventure I was involved in. In the summer of 1943 I was 15-years old. After finishing my shift at the Forge, as Ross's was known, and having just had my tea I found myself at a loose end so I decided to go for a walk along the canal towpath to the now derelict West Kiveton colliery. On the way I had to pass The Boatman Inn which was near a large turning point for the barges when operating, though now unused for that purpose. The water was always swarming with minnows and gudgeon, small fish ideal for children to catch, and of course this attracted many children of mixed ages to the area.

This particular afternoon my nephew David Lindley was there with a few friends. As I got to within 15 yards of them David fell into the water. Normally this would have been no problem, but he had gone in where there was an underwater run-off drain and it was open and was sucking him down. He was a slightly built 7-year old, so I leapt in and held him above the water level until help came to pull him out. The help was in the form of two adults, one being Mrs Swift, a schoolteacher. She wanted to send a record of this somewhere to obtain an award for me, but my guardians said no, which I too was very happy about as I did not want any fuss.

Even to this day if David and I are involved in a little leg-pulling he will often say: "Don't you wish you had left me in the canal?" to which, after a long period of imaginary thought, I answer "No".

Now back to the bike. As I said, it was a top class cycle and no mistake. It was so light it could be lifted with one finger under the crossbar. It had up-to-the-minute 4-speed gearing, and the seat! What can be said about it? Let me put it this way, I had seen thicker carving knife blades, so that if you thought I walk a little strangely, now you have the answer.

On my first week's holiday at the Forge my young workmates and I decided that instead of hanging about on the streets all week we would cycle to, no not Cleethorpes, no not Skegness, but BLACKPOOL! I remember facing that journey with as much fear and trepidation as the astronauts must have felt before the moon landing.

The journey there took two days. We had tents with us and at night we not only slept in them but also rested our tortured muscles. I have no idea how many muscles the human body has, but I can assure you every one of mine gave me agony. We spent a day and a half in Blackpool then 'home James and do not spare the pedals'. It took me two and a half days to complete the run back home, it took nearly two weeks to recover from that ordeal, for that is what it was. Needless to say, that was one cycle ride never to be repeated by me.

12. Adolescence and early Teens

As a handsome 16-year old (that by the way is only my opinion which I stand by), I could not afford to go out every night, so all week my friends and I would limit our spending in order to have a good weekend.

On Saturdays we enjoyed the choice of going to the cinema at Killamarsh or to Eckington, which boasted of having two picture houses. The Electra cinema stood nearly opposite where today's post office now stands, and on the second floor was a billiard room which had twelve tables. The so-called 'bottom pictures' was to the rear of the new billiard hall on Peveril Road.

The highlight of the week was on Sunday night in Eckington. At least one hundred plus teenagers from Killamarsh, Beighton, Barlborough and Renishaw would descend on Eckington on Sunday evenings and as there were no cinemas open on Sunday nights, I can understand you being perplexed as to why all these young people would gather in this village. Well, they collected on what was fondly known as the 'monkey run', please do not ask me to explain why it was so-called, because I do not know.

It had suddenly come to our knowledge that girls were not as annoying as we had thought, and the girls decided that the boys were not as loud and smelly as they had imagined, so we all gathered in this spot to acquaint ourselves of this discovery. The 'monkey run' was a stretch of pavement directly opposite the Drill Hall, which is next to the Army Cadet building, on a straight piece of road maybe 500 yards long. It may seem odd but all we teenagers did was to walk to one end of the road then turn round and walk back the other way. Of course that is not the whole story, on the way in either direction we would pause and chat to the girls or reminisce with friends, or just get to know other people who were doing the same as us.

It would be a waste of time to say the police turned a blind eye to all these teenagers gathered in such a small area, their thinking was spot on. However, all they did was observe our behaviour and if too large a crowd did gather they would ask us to move on which we did. It should be said the police were polite in the way they asked us to move on so there was no animosity on either side. If everything was in order the police constable went up to the shopping area but often returned later. Whilst talking of the shops, I know of some occasions when some couples who were feeling a bit amorous and who had retired into a shop doorway would end up having a bucket of water thrown over them by an irate shopkeeper. Sometimes I thought it was not necessary to go that far, anyway I suppose that dampened their ardour somewhat.

The problem was maybe some unsuspecting person could receive the same treatment, I suppose the old adage 'Tar and Brush' springs to mind at this point. Many teenage romances started on the 'monkey run' and some developed into stronger relationships. What I can say with certainty is that no serious trouble erupted on Sunday nights, and I for one will never regret having a stroll down the 'monkey run' to see what 'talent' there was to get to know.

Apart from the cinemas, on most Saturday nights a dance would be held in the Drill Hall in Eckington which I mentioned earlier and local dance bands would supply the music. On my first visit I discovered what was meant by the word wallflower, due to my inability to dance, there was no waving your arms in the air and twitching your rear end, the gentleman was obliged to hold the lady round the waist with one hand and hold one of her hands with your other hand, now that is dancing!

So my answer to this was to enrol in Mr Whewell's School of Dancing (no relation to the fishmonger), the venue being the Miners Welfare in Killamarsh. After a few lessons my attitude was, look out Fred Astaire here I come, although a few ladies thought differently as they bathed their sore toes. Another thing worth a mention is the fact that apart from the odd drunk, it was always a good night out.

One sport I really enjoyed was roller-skating which at that time was a very popular sport. The skating rink my friends and I used was situated on Attercliffe Road in Sheffield, amazingly it had escaped damage during the blitz on the city. When I was serving with the army in Egypt some of my comrades and I would visit a town at the side of the Suez Canal by the name of Ismailia which boasted of a fantastic rink. But we could only use it in the evenings as apart from our duties it would be too hot for anything as energetic as that during the day. Swimming was the in thing in the heat of the day, our base was in Fayid which was very close to the Bitter Lakes which formed part of the Suez Canal and was great to swim in.

But I am getting ahead of myself. Before ever I experienced the heat of Suez, there was the English winter of 1947 to endure.

In December 1946 I received my call-up papers to join His Majesty's forces. My first unit was the Royal Leicestershire Regiment based at South Wigston barracks near Leicester. I was ordered to report there on 18th January 1947. On that day it started snowing and continued on and off throughout my induction training, so not only had we to contend with the elements but our sergeant as well.

An entry in my P45 or pay-book gives a report on my shooting abilities as follows: Private Dye 19127408 obtains an excellent 9 out of 10 on both rifle and bren, achieved 'in inclement weather.' We were firing at targets in the middle of a snowstorm for goodness sake!

Yes, I am aware that wars are fought in all weathers.

After my initial training I was graded and posted to the Royal Signals training establishment, Bourlon Lines, Catterick Camp, North Yorkshire. I was to be taught how to be a competent wireless operator on what was fondly known as 'the back breaker'. This was a radio designed for communicating between the front line and headquarters. My problem with these sets was that they were portable, meaning that I was obliged to have it strapped to my back. It may be worth a mention that I only weighed between eight and nine stones, so this radio felt as heavy as I was.

Anyway, back to the snow. Whenever we were on training exercises the locals looked on us as some kind of nutcases, there we were crawling about in deep snow with radios on our backs. We understood why they would think that as we also shared these thoughts.

But things were getting worse for outlying villages which were not receiving any supplies due to the condition of the ice-bound roads. The army was called in to assist as they had transport that could cope better with the snow and ice: tracked vehicles and four-wheel drive trucks. We delivered coal and food supplies to these people for weeks, with the emphasis on the elderly and disabled. At times it was heart-rending to receive their gratitude. They would try to ply us with money and gifts, we had difficulty refusing and telling them we were only doing our duty. But we did not look on this as a duty, we thought of it as an honour to serve.

I was granted a 48-hour pass to visit home. All the rail links to Sheffield were closed due to snow and ice, but the Chesterfield line was still accessible so off I went. Once in Chesterfield I caught a bus to Killamarsh and after quite a few skids and near misses with other vehicles we arrived at the bottom of Spinkhill Lane. The bus tried to get traction to get up the sloping road and failed, so a gentleman and myself got out of the bus and, one on each side of the vehicle, proceeded to throw pieces of hawthorn, elder or any sort of growth under the drive wheels to keep it moving which we succeeded in doing all the way up the lane to the Roman Catholic School in Spinkhill village. After this it progressed without our help for which the gentleman and myself were truly grateful as we were completely shattered.

Killamarsh was virtually cut off by snowdrifts as I had to walk from where Westthorpe Road joined Spinkhill Lane, and most of the minor roads were impassable. Ashley Lane looked non-existant as the snow was level with the top of the hedges. Bread and other goods had to be collected from the bottom of Station Road by the shopkeepers dragging sledges and prams.

This was the time that the horse and cart came back into favour. The engine-powered, rubber-wheeled transport had met its match in the snow and ice. The farmers of the village became the heroes of the hour by loaning out their horses and tractors, but also by supplying milk as milk from outside was reduced to a trickle. Bramhalls of Bridge Street had never sold as many shovels as they did in 1947.

The Gascoigne brothers, farmers, did their best to keep the roads of Killamarsh clear being owners of two snowploughs. One was a great heavy wooden V-shaped artifact with the underside covered with metal plates where the plough made contact with the road. This plough needed two horses to pull it at times, depending on the volume of lying snow. The smaller one was used, surprise, surprise, for clearing snow from the pavements or footways. I say surprise because today's pedestrian has to put up with icy or snow-covered footpaths.

This difficulty stayed with us until late April. The people say that the summer of that year was the warmest they could remember. My comment to that was that I knew nothing of it as I had been posted to Port Suez in Egypt which was even warmer!

I should stop this now as I am starting to drift away from my boyhood. At this point tribute must be paid to the group of people who influenced my life as a boy, and as I matured into adulthood.

First and foremost must be my aunt and uncle, Polly and Alfred Evans, who brought me out of the care home and lavished all their love and care on me in all the stages of my life. I am aware that this next statement will sound selfish but it is not meant that way. They could not have children of their own, so I enjoyed the benefits of their misfortune or I may have been writing another story.

Next come my boyhood pals, Roy Hughes a more steadfast friend does not exist. If we had a squabble I would call him Ginger nut as he had the reddest hair I have ever seen, he called me skinny Dye alluding to my puny physique. Sadly he passed away in his thirties. Next comes

Granville Cramp, 'Crampy', he had a very harsh upbringing due to extremely strict parents, my opinion is that his happiest times were when he was in our company, if I am wrong he will correct me as he lives next door to us with his wife Joyce.

Leslie Clarke, the only thing I can say of him is that he was as mad as a 'March hare'. He would tackle anything for a laugh. Leslie died over twenty years ago. Roland Spooner another friend who had a rough boyhood also passed away. Harold Laws very dependable, if he said anything he meant it. He is now a District Councillor as well as Parish Councillor.

Richard 'Dick' Barlow, he was the quiet one among us, he lived with his mother and his siblings in Nethermoor Lane. They all had a hard life due to the fact that his father had been killed in 1934, in an accident at Kiveton Colliery, but you must understand that that the family had a loving and caring mother who stuck by them through good and bad times but they were mostly bad as she struggled to bring them all up. I can remember that when I was in Richard's company his waif of a sister Margaret would always be hovering around as if she was missing something. Anyway I thought she was a bit of a pest then quite suddenly, or so it seemed, she matured into this beautiful young woman overnight. Inevitably we fell in love and I married my long term sweetheart nearly 60 years ago and I ask myself where have all the years gone?

Whilst referring to Richard I feel compelled to tell you this, he did me the honour of asking me to be best man at his marriage to Brenda Bradder of Eckington, but the powers that be intervened and had my demobilisation delayed for six months due to the shortage of wireless operators in Egypt at that time. You can imagine my disappointment at having to miss the chance to do the honours for my greatest pal.

Still on the subject of my Army career, after finally being demobbed and getting married and settling down to civilian life, I was still on the reserve list. At this time the Korean war was raging and I was summoned to attend a medical examination in Mansfield prior to call up. In the interview before the medical I was asked if I was married to which I replied "Yes", when were you married? I replied on the 2nd of September

1950, have you any children? "Yes one boy", when was he born? On the 3rd of September 1950, I had to hurriedly correct that answer to 1951 or it would have meant that Margaret had only been married 24 hours before giving birth to our son Michael.

After this everything began to go pear-shaped, the room in which my examination was held must have been the smallest room in the building, the room boasted a very large desk, at which sat a sour-faced female doctor, she came to the front of the desk and proceeded to examine my naughty bits with a wooden spatula, it could be said that this was the first time I had been on a perch!

She then went back and sat down behind the desk, I was told to touch my toes with my fingers which was no problem, but what I had not noticed that fixed to the wall behind me was one of those large cast-iron radiators, as I bent forward to touch my toes my rear end caught the extremely hot radiator, causing me to leap forward and the room being so small I ended up halfway across the doctor's desk, take note I still was not wearing any clothing at all, and I must say that I have never seen so much fear cross a person's face as crossed that doctors, I suspect she was thinking she faced a fate worse than death, 'as they say' but she had no reason to fear as I could not vacate that room fast enough. I should stop now as I could reminisce forever.

13. My final word

After my initial hiccup regarding my father and stepmother, and of course leaving the care home (I would welcome any help in finding the home), once in Killamarsh I can say that my life really began to take shape.

From that time on, as I see it, my parents were Mr and Mrs A. Evans. When I was old enough to realise how good they were to me,

Polly and Alf Evans. Contentment after a job well done!

I wanted to call Aunt Polly and Uncle Alf, Mum and Dad, but they said it would be detrimental to my birthmother, so I was obliged to keep on calling them aunt and uncle.

But over the years if anyone earned those titles they certainly did, after they had passed away I always told everyone that as far as I was concerned they were my Mum and Dad, and much to my sorrow they were not there to argue the point.

After aunt and uncle must come Brother Leslie who risked a lot to get me away from my life of misery even though his life was no better. He never did disclose the repercussions following his brave and generous act of financing my get-away. Sadly he passed away in his early sixties. 'God Bless.'

Next it would be a great honour for me to say a heartfelt thank you to Killamarsh and its people for the way the village adopted me and helped me to fit in, because in a small village like Killamarsh was at that time, there was usually a fitting in period, but I can say that I was accepted from the moment I stepped off that bus on the first day.

And another thing, in all my years in the village I never heard any disparaging remarks about my parentage or my bringing up, there is a saying that goes as follows, the sins of the father shall be visited on his sons, but this was not so in my case.

Now as I approach 81 years I cannot thank the village, the people and my closest friends, not forgetting my ever loving wife Margaret.

Thank you Killamarsh.

Killamarsh Hall
(Courtesy of Derbyshire Records Office)

A Village History

A Peek into the Past

Introduction

We have, as far as possible, attempted to find factual incidents and searched records to relate in this book. Our task has not been made any easier by the scarcity of information on the time before the Angles settled here. For instance we do not know of any Neolithic sites in the immediate area of Killamarsh, if there were any they have been lost to us for many years.

The scant knowledge we have of Neolithic people are the animal bones and smoke blackened roofs of the caves at Cresswell which show us that they once inhabited Cresswell Crags. This site lies only 7 miles from Killamarsh and is the only site in Britain where Neolithic paintings have been found. It is already famous in the archaeological world, and is a major tourist and educational attraction. The management have been working towards a title of World Heritage status and hope to achieve this within 2 or 3 years.

There was an Iron Age settlement at Beighton just over the border in South Yorkshire. Evidence of this is in the form of the top of a pair of stones used for grinding corn. The top half, known as the Beehive Quern Stone because of its shape dates from 25AD and was found in a ditch by Mr G. Mirfin in Robin Lane, Beighton and was placed in the Sheffield Museum in the 1950s, the bottom half has never been found. In about 50AD the Romans introduced the flat quern stone, replacing the beehive shape and thus helping us to date the Beighton stone.

The Romans are said to have been in the village of Killamarsh which, if the story is true, did not bear this name; however there is no evidence of this. The nearest evidence we have of Roman habitation was found at Kiveton which is only three miles to the north of our village. Shards of pottery, a corn drying kiln and a corn mill, were found between Kiveton and Harthill so the chance of the Romans being in the village is not beyond possibility. To be fair this area would not be a very hospitable place to found a sizeable settlement. It was heavily forested, animals abounded, and it was also home to the Saxons who were not on the friendliest of terms with the Romans to say the very least.

The Romans had a guard post at Harthill and used the pre-historic road now called Packman Lane; this was part of Ryknield Street which in its entirety ran from Wall near Lichfield to Templeborough or Doncaster. To the Romans this was a very important military road.

There is folklore attached to the village of Harthill which goes like this: if anyone was to see a ghostly Roman legion marching along Packman Lane war is imminent. I was told this by a miner from Harthill who was employed at the same mine as myself namely Westthorpe colliery, that his Father had witnessed this just before the First World War started. My blood ran cold when he told me this story. I have an open mind regarding ghost stories, but this one I would like to believe was true. A few years ago a metal detector operator unearthed a copper trumpet thought to be Roman from somewhere along Packman Lane, that is all the information I can obtain about this discovery.

We as a group hope you enjoy reading this book as much as we have putting it together, we also consider it a rare privilege to be able to take part in this endeavour, but we must emphasize this is a personal 'Peek into the Past' it may not ring many bells for the history buffs, but we hope it will make easy reading for the many residents of Killamarsh. It may even create a yearning to learn more about our interesting village especially among our school children.

Bernard Dye

1. Beginnings

The Angles were a Germanic-speaking people and one of the main groups to settle in Britain after the Romans. They founded several kingdoms of Anglo-Saxon England, and indeed, their name is the root of the name 'England'. They moved north in the 5th century AD following the River Don and then the River Rother in their search for land suitable for farming and capable of sustaining their families.

The ancient name for the Rother was 'Rudwhr' meaning 'red water' due to the impregnation by iron oxide picked from parts of its channel. The river rises in Pilsley and joins the River Hipper at Chesterfield then flows in a north-easterly direction to Killamarsh and the Rother Valley Country Park.

At last the Angles discovered the place they had been searching for, a wide strip of marshland beside the Rother. From this marsh the land rose in a gentle slope, rising steadily southwards. They found it ideal for their needs, and being rising ground it would be easily defensible.

The area was occupied by Saxons who were hunters not farmers. Their hunting ground, 'the Forest,' at this time stretched for some one hundred miles from Nottinghamshire to York, and was also between fifteen and thirty miles wide, and was known as Sherwood Forest. Generally speaking it was a wilderness of trees similar to those at Edwinstowe today, where the Major Oak is an outstanding specimen. There were clearances at intervals in which were small market towns which developed into Mansfield, Bolsover, Clowne, Chesterfield, Rotherham, Newark, Retford, Worksop, Maltby and Doncaster, although these towns did not necessarily bear these names at the time. There were no paved roads in the forest, but there were many tracks, mainly used by wayfarers on foot or horseback. Carts or wagons would not be used; ladies would either ride pillion or they would be carried in litters.

A traveller would have to become accustomed to seeing endless trees, in which roamed multitudes of deer, swine or boar, wolves, foxes and even wildcats. Modern place names bring these to mind: Harthill is derived from *Hart*, the old English meaning an adult deer, Todverick or modern Todwick or 'fox village' keeps this in mind for *Tod* is the old word for fox. There were various species of birdlife most of which disappeared with the destruction of the forest. This forest would not only hold these animals, but anyone who did not agree with the authorities would hide there. As well as the ne'er do wells, these were the people that in all probability the legend of Robin Hood would be based on.

Sir Walter Scott describes the forest in his story of Ivanhoe: "In that pleasant district of merry England which is watered by the river Don, there extended in ancient times a large forest, covering the greater part of the beautiful hills and vallies (*sic*) which lie between Sheffield and the pleasant town of Doncaster, here were fought many of the most desperate battles during the Wars of the Roses. And here also flourished in ancient times those bands of gallant outlaws."

Referring to Locksley, or Robin Hood as he became known in legend, Scott also talks about these outlaws quite often later in his book. "The outlaws were all assembled around the Trysting-tree in the forest at Hartill-walk where they had spent the night."

On their arrival the Angles set themselves the task of clearing far larger tracts of forest than the existing clearings to create farms to grow crops, and also to provide a large area for their cattle to have plenty of grazing.

There was an interim period where, until the crops and animals could be produced in sufficient quantities to support all their families, an alternative food source would have to be found.

At this point, into history or (local legend) stepped a person by the name of Kynwold. He was not a farmer and had taken over the aforementioned wide strip of marshland along the south side of the Rother Valley. It would have been well-stocked with wild fowl, deer and wild boar and the river teeming with fish. So the settlers took advantage of the marsh and with Kynwold's help had enough food to keep them up and running until their farms achieved self-sufficiency. To express their gratitude, so the story goes, the farmers named the settlement after him, hence 'Kynwoldsmaresc' or Kynwoldsmarsh. The village became the hub of the farming community until the Middle Ages.

The county dyke runs east to west just north of the village. This dyke formed the border between the Kingdoms of Mercia and Northumbria. Part of the dyke still exists in what is now known as the Rother Valley Country Park. The Anglo Saxon Chronicles of 827AD tell us Egbert King of Mercia and Eanned King of Northumbria chose a place to the west of the park where they settled their differences, (I find this a strange statement to make, does it mean a battle took place or did they sit round a table and talk?). Egbert was then declared King of England at a place called Dose (it is thought that this could be Dore). In the same year 827AD that Egbert successfully subdued his Kingdom of Mercia, he then attacked Northumbria and after they were beaten they offered him obedience and concord.

The battle of Brunenburgh in the year 937AD is thought to have taken place in and around the Rother valley area. Here, Atholston King of Wessex and Mercia fought and defeated a combined army from Northumbria, Ireland and Scotland. Some of this has to be conjecture, but evidence springs from local place names, for instance Bedgreave (*Bedgrave*) and Birley (*Burghlaw*) meaning (burial place near a fort). A lane leading from Killamarsh to Bedgreave was known as Battlefield Lane (now Barbers Lane) while a short distance away is a village called Laughton-en-le-Marthen, the word Marthen means *slaughter field*.

A large number of spurs, stirrups and battle axes were discovered in land to the north of today's Rother Valley Country Park during the planting of hedges for the enactment of the Enclosure Act of 1779. This was when common land was enclosed by hedges, mainly hawthorn or blackthorn, and it is thought that the art of hedge laying began at this time to form an impenetrable barrier to keep livestock in their owners field.

The Four Thorpes

The name Thorpes is of Viking origin meaning 'village' or 'farmstead', however, we do not imply that Vikings had been in the area of the settlement that had been awarded to the King's Thanes. The King on the throne at this time was Edward the Confessor (1042-1066) followed by the brief reign of King Harold. These Thanes were Alueld who held the Kirkthorpe manor, reputedly the richest, and Cedric, Godric and Thorgils who held Upperthorpe, Westthorpe and Netherthorpe respectively.

Thanes were the men who helped the King with finance for war, also supplying men and arms when they were required. A horse, a sack and a spur, and the horse should be to the value of five shillings, to be furnished whenever the King made war, such were the conditions under which they were allowed to hold Killamarsh. The horse and spur are self explanatory, but the sack? After quite an amount of research it seems it was a bag of coarse woven material similar to hessian it is believed the thane or knight would use it for holding his loot taken in battle.

The Normans

In 1066 came the invasion by William of Normandy and his army, who defeated and killed King Harold at the Battle of Hastings. When he had overrun all England he dealt harshly with anyone who dared to defy him.

Something of this nature must have occurred in Kynwoldsmaresc because King William, as he now was, confiscated the four Thorpes and formed them into two, giving Kirkthorpe, the richest, and its neighbour Upperthorpe to Ascuit Musard. The other two namely Westthorpe and Netherthorpe he gave to William Peveril for services rendered during the invasion of Britain. The wooden church was burned down just before 1086 in one of the many rebellions against King William.

In 1086 William ordered a great book to be compiled, its purpose was to list everything of value in his new kingdom, for example, woodland, pasture and land arable. This book was named Domesday Book and Chindwoldmaresc is listed in it. The pages shown have Latin on one side and opposite is the interpretation of these words. Take note how the value of the Thorpes had dropped after William had given them to his favourite Knights.

Also included is an explanation of how the name Chinewoldmaresc evolved into Killamarsh over the years. You may be puzzled as to why the spelling of the village changed from Kynwoldsmaresc to Chinewoldmaresc. The second name dates from after Domesday as the Normans did not use the letter K, instead they used the letters CH, and although the spelling is different the pronunciation is the same.

In about 1195 the male side of the Musard line died out, and the heiress married Mathew de Haversegg who was of Anglian descent. The Peveril manor descended through the de Herez to the de Meynells and the heiress of that family married the second de Haversegg in 1228, so after about two centuries all the manors came back into English ownership once again.

1 M. In BARLOW Hakon had 2 parts of 1 c. of land taxable.
    Land for ½ plough.
        6 villagers and 1 smallholder now have 1 plough.
        Meadow, 2 acres; woodland pasture 1½ leagues long
           and 8 furlongs wide.
    Value before 1066 and now 10s. Hascoit Musard holds it.

2 M. In STAVELY Hakon had 4 c. of land taxable. Land for 4 ploughs.
    Hascoit now has in lordship 3 ploughs.
        21 villagers and 7 smallholders have 4 ploughs.
        A priest and a church; 1 mill, 5s 4d; meadow, 60 acres;
           woodland pasture 1½ leagues long and as wide.
    Value before 1066 and now £6.

3 M. In HOLME, WADSHELF and BRAMPTON Dunning had 10½ b. of land
    taxable. Land for 12 oxen.
        8 villagers and 5 smallholders now have 3 ploughs.
        Meadow, 3 acres; woodland pasture 1½ leagues and 1
           furlong long and 2½ furlongs wide.
    Value before 1066, 20s; now 10s. Hascoit holds it.

4 M. In BRAMPTON and WADSHELF Branwin had 7 b. and 4 acres of
whose? land taxable. Land for 1 plough. Now in lordship 1 plough.
        3 villagers and 1 smallholder have 1 plough.
        Meadow, 5 acres; woodland pasture 1½ leagues long
           and 3 furlongs wide.
    Value before 1066 and now 10s. Hascoit holds it.

5 M. In KILLAMARSH Alfwold had ½ b. of land taxable. Waste.
        Meadow, ½ acre; woodland pasture 1 league long
           and 30 perches wide.
    [Value] before 1066, 16d; now 12.

13   **LAND OF GILBERT OF GHENT**

1 M. In ILKESTON, HALLAM and STANTON (-by-Dale) Ulf Fenman had 6 c.
    and 6 b. of land taxable. In BREASTON, jurisdiction. 2 c.
    of land taxable. Land for 8 ploughs and 6 oxen. Now in
    lordship 3 ploughs
        10 Freemen with 2 c. of this land; 18 villagers and
           7 smallholders who have 12 ploughs.
        1 mill site; meadow, 70 acres; woodland pasture 1 league long

Extracts from the Domesday Book

5 villagers now have 2 ploughs.
Meadow, 20 acres; woodland pasture 9 furlongs long
and 3 furlongs wide.

K   Value before 1066, 21s 4d; now 22s 8d.   d
Fulk holds it from Roger. Ernwin claims it.

3 M. In BEIGHTON Swein had 6½ b. taxable. Land for 1½ ploughs.
However, there are 4 ploughs and
11 villagers and 2 smallholders.
[Value] formerly 20s; now 32s.
Roger holds it and Leofwin from him.

4 M. In DORE Edwin [had] 2 b. of land taxable. Land for ½ plough.

5 M. There also Leofwin [had] 2 b. of land taxable. Land for 1 plough.
[Value] formerly 20s; now 64d.

6 ²/M In NORTON Godiva and Bada had 12½ b. of land and 8 acres of land.
Land for 2 ploughs.
3 villagers have 1 plough.
Ingran holds from Roger. [Value] formerly 20s; now 18d.

7 M. In ALFRETON Morcar had 4½ b. and 4 acres of land taxable,
as a manor. Land for 1 plough.
9 villagers and 3 smallholders with 2 ploughs.
Meadow, 5 acres.
[Value] formerly 20s; now 30s. Ingran holds from Roger.

8 M. In ROWTHORN Ulf and Steinulf had 1 c. of land taxable as a manor;
in BRAMLEY 2 b. of land, of Rowthorn jurisdiction.
Land for 2 ploughs.
6 villagers with 1 smallholder have 1 plough.
In lordship 1 plough; meadow, 2½ acres.
[Value] formerly 20s; now 16s.

17   LAND OF THE KING'S THANES   278 c

1 ²/M. In BARLOW Leofric and Uhtred had 2½ b. of land taxable.
Land for 5 oxen.
3 villagers and 4 smallholders now have 1 plough.
Woodland pasture 3 leagues long and 4 furlongs wide.
Value before 1066 and now 6s. 8d.

2 ³/M. In KILLAMARSH Godric, Edric and Thorgils had 7½ b. of land taxable.
Land for 1 plough.
5 villagers now have 1 plough.
Meadow, 7 acres; woodland pasture 3 leagues long
and 5 furlongs and 70 perches wide.
Value before 1066, 18s; now 9s.

Extracts from the Domesday Book

2. 1230 Growth Starts

Throughout the Middle Ages Killamarsh was basically self-sufficient in its farming and dairy products. Wild fowl from the marsh and fish from the river would vary the diet. The woods provided fuel and building materials and in places the ground yielded stone and the first small quantities of coal.

Each manor had its valuable corn mill, and the manor at Netherthorpe was the fortunate possessor of a forge for the manufacture of weapons and farm implements. The materials for ironworking were obtainable locally: pockets of iron ore would be easily dug and there was plenty of wood to make the charcoal required for smelting. There was swift running water to turn the giant wheels working all the machinery including the bellows which provided the forced draft for the furnace. Once enough coal was available charcoal was not needed in such quantities.

The land use in the village would have been on the open field system, meaning the villagers were allocated strips of land in several fields. If anyone stepped out of line, by this one assumes if they tried to usurp another peasant's land, or they did not grow the crop they were expected to grow, they would be penalised. Villagers were also allocated grazing rights on common land.

Although the Enclosure Act in 1779 caused trouble in other parts of the county, in Killamarsh enclosure had in effect been going on since the 14th century, as very gradually local landowners had been buying or taking over land that was not producing the income they thought it was capable of, due in the main to less efficient medieval farming methods.

In 1777 before the Enclosure Act came into being, the Parish awards were made. This document showed the common land and also land that had been given to various people. So when the Act came into force there were just under 400 acres to enclose in Killamarsh. Most of this land was at Highmoor and was not good quality farmland, the reason being that it fell rather steeply to the north and west and could only be used for animal husbandry. So it was utilised as such and a few small animal farms were set up around Highmoor and Pebley.

The Cruck Barn at Westthorpe

The oldest known building in Killamarsh still in existence is the cruck barn. Crucks are curved timbers used as the main framing of a building, and were always similar in shape. The ancient way of obtaining these timbers was for the carpenter to search for a suitably shaped tree, fell it and then split the tree down the middle creating two more or less identical crucks.

Often these crucks would stand on the ground but in many cases they would be placed on brick pillars. Fixed at the top was a tie beam to support the roof. This set-up was sometimes called an 'A' frame.

Barns built by this method evolved in the Saxon age, but came into their own in medieval times. The barn in our village used three trees, creating six crucks in all. The crucks were open to the elements for a number of years after which side walls and gable ends were added. It was then divided into three parts, one part would be for the family living quarters, the middle part housed the cattle and the third section was used for the storage of provender, this part was also used for threshing grain.

This barn in Killamarsh has now been renovated and all the building has been converted into a modern home, with this proviso, that all materials used on the outside of the building had to be exactly the same as were used in the original construction, even the constituents of the mortar had to conform to the ancient standards.

Anyone interested in this type of barn could visit Barlow Woodseats manor house in Derbyshire which is reputed to have in its grounds the longest cruck barn in the county and possibly in the United Kingdom.

(Information obtained from the book 'English Historic Carpentry' by C.A. Hewitt ISBN 0 85033 3547)

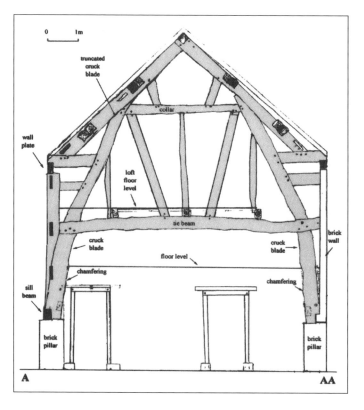

Cruck barn construction.
Note that in this drawing the topmost timbers have been machine cut to replace rough-hewn earlier timbers.
(From English Historic Carpentry by C.A. Hewitt)

3. Coal Mining, Canals and Railways

Coal was becoming more and more important in the late 16th and early 17th centuries. The Dales, which were part of the land which was too steep to farm, were ideal for 'footril mines', or in the modern idiom, 'drift mines'. The adits or entrances would be driven into the steep banks (more of this later).

Meanwhile something more fundamental was happening to the general landscape of the village. Bell pits were appearing all over the village. Operated by whoever owned the land, bell pits took their name from the shape of the shaft. The excavation was a wide shaft topped by a set of headstocks to carry the pulleys for the winding rope. Once the coal seam was reached the mineral would be taken out, and the miners would then excavate round the circumference at the bottom of the shaft thus forming the bell shape.

The shaft would be supported by wooden spars, at the same time making sure that the tub could be lifted and lowered without fouling these timbers. Wooden props were used to support the roof as the miners undercut the sides of the shaft. This was a very hazardous occupation indeed. There would have been very little ventilation and the lighting was primitive.

The coal was brought to the surface by what was called a Horse Gin. Usually two horses were tethered to bars which were connected to a large drum. The winding rope was wound round the drum and from there it went over the headstocks pulley and then the rope was fastened to a tub which was used to lift and lower the miners up and down the shaft, and to bring the coal to the surface.

There were limits as to how far the miners could undercut the bottom of the shaft, the stability of the strata above the coal seam governed this. The manager or owner would decide on the limit that coal could be excavated safely. After the mine was exhausted another shaft would be sunk close by. The overburden from the new shaft would be used to backfill the disused mine. Evidence of this type of mining can still be seen in the Dales as a series of circular depressions marking the sites of the old shafts.

Now to be more specific regarding the footrils mentioned earlier. Two tunnels were driven into the steep bank, and one of them would have a vertical shaft driven down to it. The tunnels were joined together and a series of air-tight doors were set in place. At the bottom of the shaft a large fire would be lit and the draught caused by the fire would draw fresh air round the workings providing a reasonable ventilation system. As with all mining at this time the drawback would be primitive lighting, the miners of the day had to work by the light of a candle or oil-lamp. The early days of mining were not for the faint-hearted.

Mining of coal in the 16th and 17th centuries was limited to more or less the local area due mainly to the state of the roads that would not allow the export of the coal to other towns and villages. Local brickworks and lime-kilns would be the main customers even though householders were turning from wood burning to coal. Eckington had its own mines, as did most of the other villages in the area, so this type of mining carried on until the late 18th and early 19th centuries.

In 1777 Derbyshire's genius James Brindley brought the Chesterfield to Stockwith Canal through the village, effectively slicing Killamarsh in two. The canal went through a tunnel a hundred yards from the border between Wales Parish and Killamarsh. The tunnel was reputed to be the longest in the country at 2884 yards (2.6 kilometres) in length and 9 feet wide (2.75 metres), but was so low that the bargees would literally walk the barge along with their feet on the tunnel roof whilst lying on their backs.

From then onwards things moved forward at an amazing speed, as the demand for coal all along the route of the canal increased, the need for coal far outstripped production due to the limited quantities the old fashioned methods allowed. So it was the industry had to modernise and fast if they were to keep all those burgeoning markets satisfied. There were competitors all along the canal eager to sell coal to the towns. Coal was also exported into Lincolnshire by means of the canal and produce was brought into the village from that county; coal was also taken to Chesterfield.

The canal continued in use until the 1870s. A man by the name of William Blackwell had arrived in Kiveton around that time to start work at the new mine in Kiveton. He also got involved with the canal and started legging the so called 'cuckoos' through the tunnel. These barges were mostly loaded with Derbyshire stone for the construction of the Houses of Parliament. One day whilst legging he heard stones dropping from the roof. That signalled the end of the tunnel, as the collapse was imminent. The tunnel was closed for safety reasons and finally it collapsed nearly halfway along in 1907.

However, until its closure, the canal had been the spur for the development of coalmining in the area. A deep mine was sunk at Halfway by the name of Holbrook Colliery by the Sheepbridge Coal and Iron Company. Another colliery shaft was sunk on the border of Wales Parish and Killamarsh to the rear of the Angel Inn on Gander Lane now Rotherham Road, and was named the Norwood Colliery by the same company.

Norwood colliery shaft went down to the top hard seam which lay at the depth of 484 feet (148 metres). In 1865 production started in this seam, there would be other seams but we cannot find any records of these. The mine is shown to be owned by J. and G. Wells in 1925 and this company also owned Holbrook Colliery at Halfway, this from Kelly's Directory of that year. There was also a colliery along the canal towards the tunnel by the name of West Kiveton Colliery which was just inside the Wales Parish border. Both Norwood and West Kiveton mines could load their coal straight onto barges, the stonework that supported the chutes is still in evidence on the canal side.

West Kiveton Colliery, looking east.
Note the position, nearly halfway up the flight of 13 locks on the canal.

These three mines (Holbrook, Norwood and West Kiveton) attracted hundreds of miners and their families from other coalfields, and one has to ask why? Were the wages better, had the working conditions improved, or were the coal seams running out elsewhere? We must try to imagine how the population swelled in the village, lodgings must have been at a premium, the brickworks would be working flat out to produce the bricks required for the housing boom. In fact it must have been a shot in the arm for many business enterprises as well as the shopkeepers of the village.

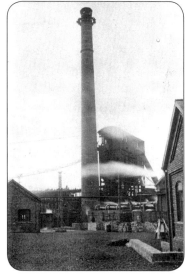

Norwood Colliery to the rear of the Angel Inn.
The colliery closed in 1943.

Norwood Colliery was a very profitable enterprise according to records which show that at its height the mine was producing in the region of 600 to 700 tons of coal per shift daily. Its 4,000 tons per week was a good share of all the production of all the mines in Killamarsh which was 10,000 tons per week. Norwood mine eventually closed in 1943.

Three smaller mines were operating at Highmoor. Highmoor Colliery was owned and run by the Greensmith family, on the opposite side of the road where the modern day Highmoor drift-mine was situated; the other two were the Comber and the Comberwood mines. These three mines Highmoor, Comber and Comberwood loaded their coal into tubs and it would be taken on rails through the Dales to a spur of the canal at the bottom of Churchtown called the Carole or Curr-hole. Some of the iron rails in the Dales are still in place, but are so overgrown it would be difficult to locate them without the help of a metal detector. The Carole was filled in many years ago to protect children from the danger of drowning.

This coal was won at a terrible price in human lives. There were safety rules in place but a lot of the time they were ignored in the rush to improve production. Below are just a few of the victims of accidents in the Killamarsh area.

On January 6th 1858, Richard Turton, William, John and Frank Senior were all killed when the rope holding the tub they were in broke and the tub crashed to the bottom of the shaft of the Perseverance mine at the top of Nethermoor Lane. Thomas Hutchby died in an accident at Norwood Colliery, date not available at this time, his widow and two children stayed on in the village, she opened a beer-off shop at the bottom of Bridge Street and later on the opposite side of the street she opened a salt factory.

On November 22nd 1871 George Barthop was killed instantly in an explosion at Norwood Colliery and many more were injured. Of these men eight died later suffering severe burns; these figures were obtained from Derbyshire Times records. In January 1872 John Severn and Bill Mellorship died in accidents at Norwood, they had only just moved into the village from another mining area. There were also many injured miners suffering broken limbs etc. Too many names to remember, too many tragedies to relate, as was said earlier the miners paid a heavy price, winning the coal that created so much wealth, but not for them. We in the village think that they were the bravest of men and there can never be enough memorials to their deeds.

And let us not forget their families who had to endure hardship and poverty. Yes we say poverty, because mining bosses kept wages as low as possible to stick to their profit margins. If the worker had the temerity to complain he would be dismissed on the spot, and if the family were unlucky enough to live in a company house they were forced to quit immediately as no notice would be offered.

Things began to improve in the miners' place of work as new safety rules were brought in, and new mining methods were introduced, for instance the compressed air tools that came into use in 1860. Compressed air was also used to power coal-cutting machines, making the getting of coal easier. The noise created by this type of machine was horrific, even so it gave a boost to output per man shift. Electricity was made safe to be used underground, and in 1890 would begin to power coal-cutting machines, boring machines and most importantly belt conveyors thus making mining less labour intensive. This also meant that the use of ponies for haulage could be cut back, but not completely, some ponies were still used in some mines in the 1950s although not in Killamarsh.

The drawback to these machines was the coal dust that settled in parts of the mine with poor ventilation, for example old workings and the return airway, the stale air tunnel after it had travelled along the face and was heading in the direction of the surface. Dust also settled under the rollers on the belt conveyors so these had to be kept as clean as possible, otherwise the movement of the roller would have caused the dust to overheat dangerously. Experiments have shown that in the right conditions coal dust became a very explosive material indeed. Mining experts say many of the explosions attributed to the presence of gas could well have been caused by coal dust.

Water sprays were introduced on all coal cutting machines and where belt conveyors were in use sprays were installed at the delivery end bringing a huge improvement to the dust problem. The air was cleaner, less dust was being inhaled by the workers, so a small reduction in lung problems was achieved.

Westthorpe Colliery and the Railways of Killamarsh

In 1923 a shaft was sunk at Westthorpe to act as an air shaft for Holbrook colliery by J. and G. Wells. Then in 1928 the decision was taken to develop Westthorpe as a production mine. The depth of the shaft was 449ft (137 metres) down to the Deep Soft seam. Coal would be taken from this seam for the next twenty years, and whilst production in this seam was going on plans for the future were put into place. Drifts were driven down to the Thorncliffe seam, on the way down the Parkgate seam was exposed and it was decided to exploit the Parkgate until the Thorncliffe was ready for production. The miners struggled to maintain production in the Parkgate seam due to limited height and 'washouts'. A washout means that the coal seam thinned out so much it was impossible to win mineral here so the miners were forced to use explosives to blast their way forward until the seam regained its normal thickness. This was a time-consuming and very expensive operation so as soon as the Thorncliffe was ready the Parkgate was abandoned. The new Thorncliffe would produce coal for twenty years.

When both the Deep Soft and Thorncliffe seams were nearly exhausted the management took the decision in 1968 to drive drifts up from the Deep Soft workings to the Chavery seam. This seam was developed in 1970 and the first production face came into service in 1971 and the Chavery seam served Westthorpe until closure in 1984. All the faces in this seam were fully mechanised with steel Crawley conveyors in conjunction with Trepanner cutting and loading machines. These machines would straddle the conveyor and the mineral would pass under the machine as the coal headed for the surface. Hydraulic chocks were used to support the roof and were moved forward as the face advanced, these faces would be at least 656ft or (200 metres) long. National and local output records were broken time after time.

Highmoor Drift Mine was opened in 1957 on an old opencast site, this mine also broke national production records but was to close in 2002 and after a period of more open casting, the site was restored back to greenbelt land. The closure of these two mines literally tore the heart out of the village and to some extent the surrounding area.

This is a list of managers since production started at Westthorpe.

Mr. H. Kendall 1927-1943

Mr. E. Thompson 1943-1947

Mr. G. Walker 1947-1960

Mr. P. J. Griffiths 1960-1962

Mr. H. Glasby 1962-1966

Mr. A. Wheeler 1966-1967

Mr. J. Rodgers 1967-1970

Mr. C.A. Heeley 1970-1972

Mr. J. White 1972-1975

Mr. K.P. Hess 1975-1983

Mr. A. Vardy 1983-1984 Westthorpe closed.

Westthorpe Colliery open from 1928 to 1984.

The Railways and their relationship with Killamarsh

In the middle of the 19th century whilst all this mining was making progress, 'output wise' more and more demands were being placed on the canal which was struggling to keep pace with demand for coal from towns and cities and of course factories. Then engineers created the steam engine, some bright spark built a frame the round the engine, fitted specially shaped wheels able to run on steel rails and behold the railways were born. It was not quite as simple as that was it?

Killamarsh had three rail lines running just west of the village with a station on each line. The first station was The London, Midland and Scottish, the LMS built in 1874 and closed to passengers in 1954. The line is still used today but only for freight. The station does not exist anymore but the line runs under the road about 100 yards to the east of the entrance to Cow Lane.

In 1892 came the London North Eastern Railway, the LNER. The station for this company was on the aptly named Station Road, and was used extensively as a commuter line by the people of Killamarsh employed

London and North Eastern Railway (LNER) station at the top of Station Road. The station closed in March 1963.
(Photograph courtesy www.picturethepast.org.uk)

in producing munitions in Sheffield during wartime. It was also popular for people if they needed to do any shopping outside the village. The LNER closed in 1963, the station buildings are still in evidence but are used for the sale of memorabilia from yester-year. The third station, also built in 1892, was situated at Old Hall Farm and was operated by the Lancashire, Derbyshire and East Coast Railway, the LDEcR The name of this line tells us that it was popular with passengers wishing to visit the east coast resorts for day trips or longer. No trace of this station exists, it was closed in 1939.

LMS, sometimes known as the Midland Station.
First opened in February 1840, closed January 111843. It re-opened as LMS in1873 and the station closed in February 1954.
The line is still open for through traffic.

Each of these lines had a spur line to deal with the collieries' coal output. From these lines coal would be transferred to the main line and then transported to all points of the country.

Even before the roof became unsafe, the canal was folding under the dominance of the railways. Waterways were slow as opposed to rail and were suffering losses due to the tonnage these immensely powerful machines could haul and deliver much faster and to order.

Lancashire, Derbyshire and East Coast Railway (LDEcR).
The station situated at the top of Station Road, near Old Hall Farm,
was closed in 1939.

4. Steam and Electricity

With the coming of the machine age everything that needed power to operate began to be converted to steam power. In the mining industry steam engines were used for hauling wagons on the surface, and engines powered by steam were used to lift coal as well as miners to the surface.

Steam engines were also the answer to the problem of water in the mines as they could power more efficient pumps, and they could not have arrived at a more opportune moment. Water was a big problem in the mines in Killamarsh, which benefited greatly from the pumps, as some faces were subject to flooding and thereby lost output. With the help of the new technology water could be kept under control thus the output of coal would continue to increase.

Even in the 1920s steam-powered lorries could be seen trundling up and down the roads of the village, which had probably been repaired by steam roller. However most factories were being converted to electric power which in a lot of cases would be produced by the use of steam turbines.

The railways were the longest users of steam power for their powerful engines, and rail reigned supreme for many years. The railways were mainly responsible for the demise of the canal as it could not compete with the speed and the tonnage these machines could haul.

Farmers, too, benefitted from steam and would hire the great lumbering machines to thresh grain crops at the end of summer. This method was twenty or thirty times faster and used less manpower than the old fashioned winnowing or flailing. The threshing machine also filled sacks with grain ready for transporting away for storage.

The machine age did not pass without its problems. Owners discovered that they needed less labour to produce more goods so they began to shed workers and become even more mechanised, thereby stirring up ill feeling in the communities. The results included broken machines and even riots in some places when many workers were jailed, and some were transported to the colonies. But no records of this have been found implicating the workforce of Killamarsh.

Mill Road is named after the water-powered corn mill built near the river, to take advantage of its power. This site was also occupied for many years by a forge, powered by giant waterwheels which turned the shafts operating the bellows. The forced draught was needed for the smelting process, and the waterwheels were also harnessed to power the mechanical hammers used to shape the metal when white hot.

We are led to believe that a person called William Cooper established an ironworks in partnership with John Harrison, around the late 1700s or early 1800s. It was sold in its entirety to Joseph Butler and he developed rolling mills at the forge to produce chains, shovels and spades. The forge changed hands many times during the 1800s.

Joseph Butler is credited with the invention of the container as we know it today, full wagon boxes to be lifted on to flat rail bogeys, then lifted off when they had reached their destination.

A company by the name of Penns were quality wire producers, and used the forge to produce ingots or billets to be taken elsewhere (maybe Sheffield) to be rolled into wire. Ingots or billets have been found in the canal bed.

A duo named Webster and Horsfall in 1873 produced wire at the forge which was used to reinforce the Atlantic telegraphic cable on the second attempt, which was a resounding success.

The Steelmelters Arms is reputed to have been named after the men who were employed at the forge. The forge suffered flooding for five consecutive years which could last for as much as 10 weeks at a time.

5. Roads in and out of the Village

New roads were built in the 18th and 19th centuries to cope with the extra production from the coalmines and the transport of iron and steel from Killamarsh and beyond. At the same time older roads were upgraded and renamed. Major roads were turned into turnpikes.

Parliament had created the first Turnpike Trust in 1706 and by the latter half of the 18th century turnpikes were to be found all over the country. Turnpikes allowed local people to collect tolls from road-users which were used to pay for the upkeep of the roads.

Mansfield Road was turnpiked all the way up to Mosborough and on to Sheffield; Gander Lane was turnpiked through to Rotherham. They became known as the Sheffield and Gander Lane Turnpike. Tollhouses were built at most junctions to collect the toll from anyone joining the turnpike. Chains were in place at the bottom of Shepherd's Lane, or Bridge Street as it became known after renaming in 1896, and at the end of Mill Road to collect money from anyone wishing to join the turnpike in either direction. A toll house was erected at the end of Cow Lane and one was already in place at the top of Gander Lane, renamed Rotherham Road by the newly elected Parish Council in 1896.

Roads in Killamarsh were generally in a very poor condition due to the fact that the surface consisted just of stone laid on any material, for instance clay or soil. In inclement weather these roads turned into quagmires.

In Killamarsh the problem was solved by recruiting men from the Workhouse located just over the canal bridge on Shepherd's Lane. One team would be deployed to break limestone into a workable size, which would be collected by a second team whose job was to fill in the ruts and holes. A team may have consisted of just one or two men, depending on labourers' availability.

These men were expected to work for a pittance. As an example of some of the wages, believe it or not, for breaking 20 tons of limestone men were paid just 13 shillings and sixpence. Men filling the ruts were paid 2 shillings for spreading either the broken limestone or 12 loads of cinders from the forge. The volume or weight of those cinders remains a mystery. Whichever work they did on the road repairs, it must have been a back-breaking form of employment.

6. The Churches

We are now going to study the spiritual side of the village population, so back we go through the mists of time, to the second century AD to discover the roots of Christianity in the form of a wooden cross set up on the highest point on the Ceorls-Aula, loosely meaning near the Chief's house, to let the populace know that Christianity had arrived. At this time only Saxons lived in the area.

Some time later a small wooden church was erected on this spot, and the church remained this way until the Norman Invasion in 1066. Shortly after the invasion the church was burned down during one of the many rebellions that took place in protest against the harsh treatment meted out to the village of Kynwoldmaresc.

The present church building named for St Giles was started in the 12th century and is thought to have been built by one of the Musard family to whom King William awarded the Manor of Kirkthorpe for services rendered during the invasion. The chevron design over the south doorway dates from the Normans, and the building at this time had a flat lead-lined roof.

One might think the church was named for St Giles by the Normans as the French had venerated this beloved saint for centuries.

After a great deal of research we discovered that St Giles was born in the early 7th century. His latin name was 'Aegidius' but he himself was Greek, an Athenian of noble extraction. He became famous for his piety and learning, however the fame proved to much for him, as he only wished to live his life in contemplation and obscurity. He found he could not follow his wishes in the city of Athens, but thought he had found what he was looking for in the deserts near the mouth of the River Rhone where he became a hermit for a time until his followers discovered him. Giles then moved to the Diocese of Nimes where he spent many years in solitude living on a diet of wild herbs, roots and water. His sole companion was a deer or hind, some stories state that she helped feed him with her milk.

One day, King Wamba 'a local ruler' was out hunting with his entourage in the forest when they spotted the hind and chased it into a thicket. The King shot an arrow into the undergrowth hoping to hit the hind, but on investigating he discovered he had wounded St Giles in the hand. There is a slight mystery here as there are two paintings of this event; one picture shows the arrow had pierced his left hand whilst the other work of art portrays the arrow lodged in his right hand. The penitent King spared the life of the hind and gave St Giles land on which to build a monastery which was near a town named Arles.

St Giles became the patron saint of cripples, beggars and blacksmiths. His insignia is a golden hind pierced through with a silver arrow on a green shield. His sainthood was only bestowed on him many years after his death for the many miracles he is said to have performed throughout France. St Giles was responsible for the founding of the Abbey of the Benidictine Order. He died in or around the year 710 in Septimania in Languedoc, Southern France.

In the 15th century the tower was added to our village church. In the 1800s a new high pitched roof was added and the north aisle and the vestry. That is how we find the church as it stands today.

There had been plans to build a south aisle but these were shelved, for what reason we will probably never know. In the early 1800s the only services held at St Giles were marriages and burials, conducted by curates coming to the village of Killamarsh from the giant Parish of Eckington.

In 1843 the Reverend Edward Smith became the first incumbent at St Giles. During his stay he instituted large restoration work in 1845-1846. While this was being done the medieval font went missing resulting in a new font being installed when the work was finished. The Reverend Francis James Metcalfe followed in 1887. In 1890 he discovered the medieval font in a cobbler's yard being used for soaking leather. The cobbler used the edge of the font to sharpen his leather-cutting knives, the marks of which can still be seen to this day. After recovery the font was placed in the churchyard.

Francis J. Metcalfe was succeeded by the Reverend J. Powell, then Reverend N. J. Raper. The Reverend J. Milner followed in 1930, he had the medieval font restored to its proper position in the body of the church in the 1940s. In 1957 the Reverend Cheetham took the incumbency, then Reverend P. Peterkin, followed by the Reverend Clive Hilton, and the Reverend Statham. Now we have our first female Rector, the Reverend Helen Guest, the Priest in charge of St Giles.

When visiting our beautiful church the Rector or anyone connected to the church will be only too willing to show visitors all the outstanding qualities of the building. The church is open on Saturday mornings from 9.30am to 12.30, if these times do not help please contact the Reverend Helen Guest at the Rectory and arrange a meeting or visit. On leaving the church please turn left and read the inscription on the stone tablet set into the south wall which reads as follows:

To the memory of John Wright, a pauper of this parish, who died May 4th 1747 in the hundred and third year of his age. He was of middle size, temperate and cheerful, in the trying situation of darkness, poverty and old age bore his infirmities with such Christian meekness as excited the benevolence of good men and is here recorded as an instructive lesson to others.

The Reverend Christopher Alderson B.D.P.P.P. Anno Domini 1797.

What a beautiful tribute to pay to this gentleman, it really puts my scrawl to shame. This tablet needs restoring as it deteriorating fast.

Opposite this memorial stands the Celtic cross. The bottom half of the stem is the only remnant of the original cross, it is believed to have been broken during the Reformation, the top half is a reproduction. A little further down the churchyard are the village stocks which have not been used for their original purpose for many years.

Other religious buildings in the village include a Mission Room constructed of corrugated iron sheeting which seated 300. It was built at a cost of £300 paid for by the Rev. Francis James Metcalfe and some of his friends on behalf of St Giles church, to be used as a church hall.

St Giles Mission Room, Sheffield Road.

The village had a sizeable Nonconformist population, who built many chapels. In 1852 an Ebenezer chapel was opened halfway up Shepcote Hill where Curzon Close is now. From there it was moved to the top of the hill and was built in stone, where it still stands unused opposite the Endowed School.

There were squabbles among the Methodists that led to a breakaway branch being formed on Kirkcroft Lane. They opened their new chapel in 1876 at a cost of between £300 and £400, under the name of the United Methodist Free Church. Meanwhile the other group, calling themselves the Primitive Methodists, opened a chapel on Sheffield Road opposite the Mission Room. In the 1970s the two chapels decided to re-unite and use the chapel on Sheffield Road. The now defunct chapel on Kirkcroft Lane has been converted into a private dwelling.

It is reputed that the first incumbent of St Giles the Reverend Edward Smith was not very tolerant of the chapels, but there is no evidence of this, and it has been said that the Rectors that followed got on quite well with them.

7. Parish Councils

In the past all the administration of the village would be dealt with by the Church. One of the most important events to happen for the village was the change from the vestry administration to an elected Parish Council. This move occurred in 1894/5 when the very first Parish Council was formed.

In early December 1894 a meeting took place in the Endowed School attended by a good number of residents, shopkeepers and managers of several businesses in Killamarsh. Its purpose was to elect a full council with a chair and eight other councillors.

In all there were twenty nominees for the nine posts. A show of hands was required for each nominee, and the nominees with the most votes would be elected to the council. The results were as follows:

Chair, John Tankard manager of Norwood Colliery

Vice Chair, Arthur Godber

Councillors: Joseph Edwards

Albert Robinson

George Woods

Albert Hopkinson

Thomas Spencer

George Whiting

Henry Hall.

And so, love them or loathe them, Killamarsh Parish Councils over the years have contrived to do their best for the village as they thought we would like it to be, right up to the present day.

I am a member of the present Parish Council and take great pride in continuing the work started all those years ago, even though I am a very small cog on a very large wheel.

The village the new Parish Council of 1894-95 saw is unrecognisable to the one we see today, it has grown from four small hamlets to something that must constitute a township with a population of just under 10,000 souls.

8. Schooling and Charities

In the beginning the education of the children of the parish was a very hit and miss affair. The schooling of children was governed by charities who provided pay for a teacher, with the cost to some parents being 'tuppence' (in other words 2 pre-decimal pennies). It is not known if this was for one day or one week, the value of money being what it was those days, begs us to opt for a week's teaching.

The charities which supported schools in Killamarsh are listed below: (apologies if any have been omitted)

Robert Turie left a house and a croft, the rents from these would provide for the teaching of six children to learn English. Throughout the 1870s-1880s these provided £14 per year for the Endowed School.

In 1731 John Kay donated a house on Sheepcote Hill to provide a schoolhouse, the Master and Dame to teach two children to read from the Bible. Once those two were able to read another two would replace them. It is understood that if they kept to the agreement the Master and Dame would live rent free.

In 1746 Mrs Butcher left £30, the interest from this to be used to teach four children to read and write.

In 1747 Sarah Poole or Pole left £30 pounds to the Endowed School, the interest from this to provide books for teaching three children to read and write.

In 1753 Margaret and Mary Pole of Barlborough put in trust to the Free School of Killamarsh (another name for the Endowed School), a house and several closes or sections of land, all the rents from these to go to teaching ten poor children to read and receive "Instruction on the Church Of England". Trustees would administer this charity and the funds would be for the Endowed School at the top of the hill opposite the chapel, the house mentioned in the will still stands at the foot of Quarry Road and is now in private ownership.

At this time schooling was erratic and was not compulsory. Depending on the conditions at home, if the child had found employment then schooling would be out.

In 1851 the Rutherford family lived in Nethergreen. Thomas aged 57 was a blind ex-artillery man who had served in the Napoleonic wars in Spain and Waterloo, his wife Charlotte was a teacher and their home was what would come to be known as Tommy's on Dykeside. There Charlotte Rutherford would teach children to read and write. One of those children was Richard Walker who with the rest of his family lived nearby.

When Richard reached 20 years of age he built a single storied schoolhouse on Sheffield Road near his home, this school continued in use until 1880 when the Education Act was passed. This building has now been demolished.

Old School House, Sheffield Road.

The Board School or Council School as it came to be known was designed to house 521 mixed pupils and was opened in June 1880. The Head of the Endowed School, George Watts, was appointed Headmaster and his wife Mistress; a Miss Dilks took charge of the infants.

In 1923 a new Secondary Modern School was opened across the road from the Board or Council School. The first Headmaster was Mr Gregory, followed by Mr Herbert Seston who also became Scoutmaster. He was succeeded by Mr Robert Reid who later transferred to Westfield Comprehensive School at Mosborough.

In 1981 the first stage of a new Church School on Sheepcote Road was erected, the second stage was built in 1983-84. The Endowed School and the new Church School came to be known as St Giles Church School.

There are a number of other charities in Killamarsh not related to schooling.

The charity known as Hewitt Senior's was founded by will in the year 1480, "15 shillings to be paid out of town close". After considerable research we find the meaning of this statement is that 15 shillings would be paid out of the rates of a piece of land enclosed inside the town's limits, to the poor of the village.

The charity of William Hewitt by his will dated 4th of April 1599, was £100. The interest from this would be £5 and 4 shillings to be paid out to the poor annually.

The charity of John Kay by his will in 1741 left land at Delves and Boiley. The rents were to provide loaves for ten people forever.

Henry Mirfin by his will 4th of May 1744 left money to provide clothing for the poor.

The Sarah Poole or Pole charity founded by will in 1747 left £30 to provide bread every Sunday.

The charity of John Ward by his will in 1669 left the income from a piece of land to be distributed to the poorest in the form of coins, the recipients to be chosen by the Church.

These are collectively known as the Bread Charities. Funds from these should only used for the relief of need, hardship or distress generally or individually to persons resident in the Parish of Killamarsh by making grants of money or providing, or paying for, items or services calculated to reduce hardship or distress of such persons. As times have moved on bread or clothing is no longer distributed, but the funds are still available for the above. Grants can be given to needy people and are obtainable by applying to the Parish Clerk for an application form. Once completed this would be considered by three trustees of which I have the honour to be one.

9. The 1914-18 War

The grim reaper harvested many thousands of lives from both sides in the war, however, the main reason I bring this war to your attention is to name a young man of this village who richly deserves our admiration.

He was born 16th May 1890 in a cottage just four doors up from the Steelmelters Arms in Netherthorpe Lane. His name was Fred Greaves.

Fred joined the army and at 27 years old was acting Corporal in the 9th Battalion, Sherwood Foresters when an action took place in a Belgian town by the name of Poelcapelle, east of Ypres. The platoon were attacking a machine gun stronghold, the platoon commander and sergeant were casualties, so Corporal Greaves rushed forward, went to the rear of the machine-gun nest and with hand grenades, bombed the occupants. Those who were not killed were captured, as was the machine gun.

Later in the same battle all the officers were either killed or wounded so Corporal Greaves gathered his men, threw out extra posts to withstand the heavy counterattack and opened up with rifle and machine-gun fire to back up the advance. For this act of bravery he was awarded Britain's highest honour, the Victoria Cross.

Fred died in 1973. His Victoria Cross is displayed at the Sherwood Foresters Museum in The Castle, Nottingham.

Photographs of Fred and the full story can be found on the web at Wikipedia (http://en.wikipedia.org/wiki/Fred_Greaves) so I ask you to read it and be proud to live in the same village he was born into.

Fred Greaves VC

A/Cpl F. Greaves after his VC investiture

January 1918.

Fred Greaves VC.

His medals.

Fred Greaves VC, served in the 9th (Service) Battalion, Sherwood Foresters. He and they saw service in Gallipoli, The Somme, Loos, Flanders and the last 100 days - The road to victory.

Fred Greaves VC.

With Pals and kids - France or Belgium.

This seems a strange photo. So close to the death and carnage of the war - soldiers, children and a dog.

His daughter Hazel and I have talked many times about her Dad. He seems to me to be the type of man you would want next to you whether in war or peace. An ordinary man who on 4th October 1917 at Poelcapelle did an extraordinary thing.

(The doings of the battalion on that day can be found on the war diaries page)

There are a number of stories but perhaps the one I find most interesting is -:

Fred arrived back for leave prior to his VC investiture and his uniform was somewhat the worse for wear. He was told that a new one would be provided for his date at the Palace.

On his return from Derbyshire by train, he was therefore in Civvie's. A 'lady' also on the train approached Fred and gave him a white feather !. Fred said nothing to her.

Fred was also turned down for the army when he first tried to join up. He had had a serious accident some years before and his legs had suffered. Despite this he had become a champion cyclist.

Fred was offered a commission but left the Army after the war as a sergeant.

This is the Roll of Honour for the men of our village who fell in the Great War 1914-1918:

George Henry Fields

William Smith

Hadyn Batty

Jesse Stones

Joseph Walker

Wilfred Thompson

William Shepherd

Arthur Hanson

Frederick Adams

Frank Drakett

John Frederick Taylor

Thomas Archibald Godber

Walter Whitham

Herbert William Bamborough

James William Drakett

Harry Handbury

Bertram Hall

James Farewell Hobson

William Jackson

Richard Leverton

George Albert Northridge

George Price

Richard Smith

George Henry Stones

James William Scott

George Arthur Stenton

Athol Frederick Swindell

Sam Tongue

George Henry Taylor

Frank Taylor

William Drakett

Henry Draper

Clarence Charles Elliot

John William Howe

John William Tantrum

John Mangham

John Edward Lewis

Percy Willis

Ernest Worthington

Samuel Whitfield

Charles Wilson

May all these heroes of Killamarsh rest in peace.

In the First World War the people of Killamarsh had enough to worry about with their sons at the front in France, but another tragedy occurred in the village during the winter of 1915. That November had been one of the coldest for years and the ice on the canal was thick, in fact it was deemed to be thick enough to skate on and the newspapers of the time reported with surprise that the ice was capable of bearing the weight of skaters.

On 14th November a number of young people were skating on the canal and had formed themselves into a long line, each holding on to the one in front, when the first person tripped over and fell. The others following fell on top of the first and the ice, although thick, was unable to bear their combined weight. It gave way, precipitating six of the young people into the freezing water.

Brave attempts at rescue were made by several people who, in doing so, put themselves in grave danger. Six young people were drowned that dreadful day, here are their names: Fred Northbridge aged 17, pony driver of Kirkcroft Square; Harry Milner aged 18, of Kirkcroft Square; Annie Sedgewick aged 12 of Kirkcroft Square; Mary Elizabeth Watson aged 6, again of Kirkcroft Square; Alice Reid aged 21 of Boythorpe near Chesterfield and Mary Ann Ramskill aged 18 of 6 Spa Lane, Chesterfield.

All are at rest under a group of trees at the bottom of the churchyard, just a few feet from the canal that claimed their young lives. A statement in a local paper suggested that if ladders or planks had been available to lay on the ice the death toll may not have been as heavy.

10. The Village Grows

In the period between the two World Wars the village of Killamarsh began to expand. The first large building project was in 1937 when a council housing estate was erected to the rear of Rotherham Road on the right as you pass down the road going towards the Angel Inn. This estate was built to re-house families displaced from condemned dwellings in the Brickyard or, to give it its proper name, Kirkcroft Place, just above the canal below Churchtown. Families were also moved from stone cottages on Nethermoor Lane and a few from cottages on Barbers Lane.

Just a few names to jog a memory or two: Whitlam, Bingham, Jones, Wheelhouse, Cowlishaw, Watson, Barker, Barber, Laws, Staples, Ethel Barker, Jennings, Frost, Rivington, Nettleship, Watts, Bird, Arblaster, Glossop, Draper, Gay. I am sure you, the reader, can recall many more.

Building in other parts of the village was beginning to pull the Thorpes together in as much as the village took on the look of a complete entity, instead of four separate hamlets. The inevitable price paid, however, was the loss of those beautiful green fields.

11. Feast and Fishing and Fairs

Killamarsh Feast was held on the first weekend in September. After some study of old records we find that the Feast of St Giles was also celebrated on the first of September so it can be construed from this that Killamarsh Feast was most certainly connected to St Giles' festival.

It may be attributed to the Mummers who in the 1400s would travel the countryside, visiting all the outlying villages to give enjoyment to groups of hardworking folk. The Mummers were itinerant actors, dancers, jugglers and anyone who had a talent to amuse or entertain groups of people. Their repertoire was based on the cycles of the year. For instance, in the spring the shows would have a theme of fertility be it animal or crops. If they arrived in late summer the theme would be thankfulness for the successful gathering of the harvest, and of course the new additions to the animal numbers.

The Derbyshire comedy play 'Old Tup' is said to have descended from those days. In recent times it has been decided that 'Old Tup' was unique to North Derbyshire, see pages 18-20. The type of entertainment these people provided went on for hundreds of years, but there seems to be no room now for these simple things in this world of television, computers and electronic games.

There was also a black side to the entertainment enacted at various venues in Killamarsh, for example bear, bull and badger baiting, cock fighting also took place. Quite a number of these barbaric acts took place on Netherhouse Farm. The sheer cruelty of these so-called sports were the cause of a law being put in place in 1835 making it a criminal offence to participate in any of them, but it is well known that these illegal pursuits were still being held in the more sparsely occupied parts of the village years after the act was passed.

By the 1800s the boom time for the canal was fading as its trade was being eroded by the railways. So as traffic on the canal decreased, sports fishing and boating were taking its place. The latter would fall by the wayside as the canal became neglected, but fishing reigned supreme for many years. In its heyday the canal towpath would be lined with fishermen from Norwood on the Wales border to the bridge at Bridge Street and sometimes further on towards Station Road. These fishermen would travel from Sheffield and the surrounding area as well as the locals of Killamarsh.

Pubs in the village and beyond held fishing matches with beautiful prizes for the winners. Their problem was not the match itself but vying for a vacant Saturday or Sunday to hold the match as all the other pubs would be trying to book the same weekend. The prizes for the winners were cups and medals, some of which are treasured to this day as family keepsakes.

In the early 1900s there were nine public houses and four beer-offs in Killamarsh. 'Beer-offs' were shops given a licence to sell alcohol but barred from allowing the customer to partake of the alcohol on the premises.

Every year travelling fairs visited the village and set up their swings and roundabouts, coconut shy, and the covered area to house the boxing tournament. For the children there would be donkey rides, roundabouts, flying chairs and of course 'Soak the Burglar' by throwing wet sponges at his head as it was poking through a board.

The earliest venue for the fairs was a childrens' play area opposite the Nags Head pub on the West Thorpe road side, the fair was held here for many years before moving to a field where the bungalows now stand. At the time this field belonged to Farmer George Leah of Netherhouse Farm.

In later years during the late 1920s and 1930s the Church of St Giles would hold their Sunday afternoon service at the fair.

Whilst at the fair you would meet people that maybe you had not seen since the last fair; this really was a gathering place for all the villagers. Sadly though it has passed into history now, as travelling fairs have disappeared like many other village functions.

Another event now relegated to the history books is the Summer Carnival sometimes called the May Day parade. At a date before the big day a Carnival Queen or May Queen would be chosen from the girls of the village. At the same time the Queen's attendants would be chosen, a possible number would be six girls not always the same age.

On the day the Queen and her retinue were seated on a highly decorated float donated by a local farmer and pulled by the best horse on the farm spruced up with ribbons and rosettes. These would lead the parade round the village preceded by the village band.

Each year the parade would have a different starting point: Highmoor, Westthorpe Green, Station Road or the top of Rotherham Road in fact anywhere in the village. The parade would be accompanied by contingents of Boy Scouts, Girl Guides and the Boys Brigade. At some point along the way these Boys would play their trumpets in order to give the main band a breather. Representatives of the Church of St Giles, the chapels, the Police and Firemen, in fact anyone who wore a uniform would also take part As the parade progressed round the village anyone who felt so inclined would join in the march, at times it seemed all the village was on the parade.

The Queen reigned for a full year and was expected to attend most civic and village functions, for example opening bazaars, attending civic dances and any awards ceremonies.

It is my belief that the Feast and Carnival had a unifying effect on the whole village, and gave each and everyone a sense of belonging.

12. The Second World War

The war clouds that hung over Europe were now spreading over the Channel to Britain, so we must look at the effects the conflict had on the people of Killamarsh.

To set the scene we must go back to the early 1930s to the time Adolf Hitler was making plans for the conquest of all Europe. During this time Winston Churchill kept up a constant stream of warnings to the government of the day, but he failed to convince them of the danger, in fact many called him a warmonger.

Hitler's troops marched into Austria and after no one protested he then sent his army into the Sudeten Land which formed part of Czechoslovakia with a majority of citizens speaking the German language. This caused much criticism from other countries, so Hitler stated that he had no other territorial ambitions in Europe. Everyone stepped back from the brink and settled back into their comfortable way of life. Thinking that he was not being watched Hitler then took over the rest of Czechoslovakia. And still the rest of Europe did nothing. The European powers were accused of betraying Czechoslovakia when this happened. Hitler next marched into the Ruhr with all its manufacturing capacity which had been confiscated after the 1914-1918 war as reparations. He then signed a non-aggression pact with Russia's Stalin as he had designs on taking Poland.

The British Prime Minister Mr Neville Chamberlain flew to Germany to talk peace and to try to persuade Hitler to pull his troops out of Poland which he refused to do. I am certain many of you remember the chilling broadcast made by the Prime Minister on the third of September 1939, which went as follows: " Today the British Government handed Herr Hitler a note, stating that if they did not withdraw their troops from Poland a state of war would exist between us. I have to tell you now, we have received no such undertaking, so consequently this country is at war with Germany."

There was a quiet period of a few months, that came to be known as the 'phoney war'. It was during this time that the whole population, including the people of Killamarsh, were issued with gas masks. It was feared that Germany would use poison gas as they had done in the last war, but on a much larger scale including the civilian population as well as the army.

All adults and children were obliged to have their gas masks with them at all times, even if visiting the loo. Even tiny babies were supplied with a gas mask, but their protection was an object that totally enclosed the child and the air supply was provided by an adult operating a crude hand pump. Most of the babies were terrified when they were placed inside this object, and many heart-broken mothers said they would not use this instrument of terror, but thankfully it never came to that.

I am afraid it should be said that this country was not ready for all-out war, we only had a small Air Force and Army, but the phoney war helped us to re-arm a little. Materials were in short supply so iron railings were taken down all over the village to be recycled into weapons. Not everyone was happy with this. Doctor Murray was incandescent when he returned from his surgery to find his beautiful railings gone. However he calmed down when told why they had been taken, but he did say he should have been told of the plans before the railings were cut up and taken away. There were collections of anything metallic, from aluminium pans, to old lawn mowers. Does anyone remember the pile of pans at the top of Rotherham Road? There were also waste paper drives when different streets competed to see who could collect the most.

The Mission Room was turned into what was known as The British Restaurant where anyone could purchase a quality two-course meal and a cup of tea for a shilling (in today's coinage it would be 5 pence).

After the phoney war things were going badly for our troops in France which meant that the threat of invasion loomed ever closer, in fact it looked inevitable that it would happen. So the Land Defence Volunteers were formed to back up the regular troops if the worst happened. The LDV were later renamed the Home Guard and at first they were considered figures of fun, all due to the primitive weapons and the amazing ways they had to make do with whatever there was at hand to fight with. But this was to change dramatically when people came to realise how serious the situation had become.

All the road signs in the village were removed to confuse the invaders and tank traps were set into the roads. In Killamarsh our own tank trap was set at the top of Lock Hill, outside Doctor Murray's. It consisted of steel railway lines concreted into the road with about four or five feet protruding upwards. Both carriageways were blocked with these rails in a staggered formation. To negotiate these obstacles must have been an extremely hazardous undertaking at any time but imagine having to do it in the black-out! To get through a driver would have to adopt a zig-zag manoeuvre to proceed either up or down the road. The gap was so planned that a car or bus could get through but a tank could not.

After the Battle of Britain had been decided, in our favour I might add, Hermann Goering head of the German Luftwaffe or Air Force turned the full fury of the Luftwaffe on the civilian population of the towns and cities.

Killamarsh took air raid precautions as seriously as any other village did. Black-out curtains were fitted to all windows and ARP (Air Raid Precautions) wardens patrolled the streets to make sure that no rays of light escaped past the curtains. If any light was seen the cry would be heard "put that B--y Light Out." If the householder persisted in not blacking out properly he or she faced prosecution as the authorities stated that a lighted cigarette could be seen by a German pilot from an unspecified altitude.

The schools in the village were closed for a few weeks to enable the windows and glass doors to be adorned with sticky tape in a diamond configuration to limit the damage caused by flying glass should there be a bomb blast.

In the event of an air-raid or even an air-raid warning the populace were required to take shelter in whatever form that was available and stay there until the all-clear was sounded. I think a description of an Anderson Shelter is called for at this point as this was one of the most popular shelters around at this time. This shelter, named after its inventor Sir John Anderson in 1938, was a small and cheap shelter that could be erected in people's gardens. Made from six steel corrugated curved sheets bolted at the top, and with steel sheets at either end, measuring 6ft by 4ft 6 inches wide (1.8m by 1.3m) it could protect six people, not from a direct hit but from falling masonry. These shelters were half buried in the ground and earth was heaped on top, the entrance was protected by a steel door and also an earth blast wall.

Putting the finishing touches to their shelters.
(Photograph courtesy of The Midnight Watch)

Anderson Shelters were given free to poor people, and anyone who earned more than £5 per week could buy one for £7. By the time of the Blitz over two and a quarter million were built and erected in peoples' gardens.

On the day after the raid or warning children who attended school would have lessons in the morning session and in the afternoon they were given the choice of either some sleep to make up for the night before or they could choose to read a book of their choice. It should be understood that the children at this time would possibly get seriously behind in their studies, though the teachers did their best in these very trying circumstances.

Men who were not employed in essential work such as coal mining or skilled work in the factories in Sheffield or Rotherham, and in some isolated cases farming, were conscripted into the forces leaving gaps in families that in some cases would sadly, never be filled again by that person.

I think I should place some names on paper in tribute to these young men who were called up to fight whether they wanted to or not, so here they are, my apologies for any names not printed.

G. Wheelhouse RAF

A. Sadler RAF

L. Cooper RN

R. Weston Army

G. Preston Army POW

Pte Millward Army POW

G. Clementson Army

T. Dixon Army

C. Lindley Army

Pte Thorpe Army

C. Hutchinson Army

G. Whitehead Army

L. Gaunt Army

G. Weston Army

H. Robinson Army

The ones who did not come back

K. Baker

F. Barlow

T. Bingham

F.J. Wardley

C. Perkins

A. Hipkiss

A. Barker

F. Cramp

E. Whiteley

E. Bentley

E. Stenton

A. Hopkinson

K. Davy

Alice Skinner

These are people we should be proud of as they served and some gave their all, so we would have the right to freedom and a way of life second to none.

The air raids on Sheffield brought the war uncomfortably close to us all in Killamarsh. I remember sitting in our next door neighbour's Anderson Shelter and listening to the explosions as the Germans dropped their deadly cargo on the citizens of Sheffield. At the beginning of hostilities the German radio announced that the Luftwaffe only bombed military or industrial targets. What a monstrous lie that turned out to be, we have only to remember London's East End, Coventry, Southhampton and Glasgow and many more.

I went into Sheffield after the raids to make sure my sister Doris who lived in Attercliffe was safe and well, as indeed she was. Whilst I was there she took me to parts of the city to see the damage caused by the bombing and we saw row upon row of houses flattened. They were nowhere near any factory or military base, the destruction we saw was indescribable.

It was said at the time that the bombers followed a train to Sheffield by the light of its fire box. The city was nearly always covered by a cloud of dust and industrial smoke, so the Germans had great difficulty finding it even with all their maps. It was during one of these raids on Sheffield that a bomber was damaged and had to leave the area before releasing all of its bomb load. The pilot flew over Beighton and jettisoned the remaining bombs over what is now known as the Rother Valley Country Park. When in 1977 one 2,000 pound bomb was exposed by a mechanical excavator and was exploded at 4 pm one Saturday in November, it could be said that was some delay fuse! There is another theory, that the pilot was aiming for the large rail junction at Beighton but thankfully missed. Our local poet wrote a piece about it.

As the war dragged on the people of the village became more and more involved in the war effort. The ladies of the village would hold what were known as 'Knitting Bees' to help supply our troops with winter garments such as socks, gloves, scarves and balaclava helmets.

All the village would come together to participate with every village in the area in 'Buy A Spitfire Weeks', the reasoning being that one village would take too long to collect enough money to be able to purchase a fighter plane. In the beginning a cashometer was set up in a conspicuous place. Ours would be placed at the front of the infants school on the right hand side of School Lane heading towards Lock Hill. At the top it would have our target total which would be around £1,500 to £2,000. We must remember that our village was very small in those days, and this was a staggering amount for us to collect. Over the weeks the arrow indicator seemed to be static or hardly moving at all. Collection boxes were placed in every shop in the village, dances were held in the schools or the Miners Welfare; there were fancy dress parades (now that was a

AHR BOMB.

To the strains of *'Deutchland Ube'* in the spring of *'thirty-nine'*
A bloke called Schickelgruber, ranted *"This Kampf is mein!"*
He gazed upon a great big bomb, and said, in accent harsh
"Der Englander , I'll overcome – mark that one Killamarsh,
Fix a nice slow fuse on,- delayed action, I mean,
This should cause confusion, ein nacht in t'Nethergreen!"

With true Teutonic thoroughness, the bomb that held our fate,
In *'77,* At last went off – some thirty-odd years late!

– – –

The 2,200lb unexploded bomb, found in the Meadowgate opencast site (now the
fishing-lake in the Rother Valley Park) shattered the peace on Saturday November
26th, 1977 when it was detonated by the Royal Engineers, Explosives Ordnance
Disposal, Caterham, Surrey. The five-foot 'Herman' type bomb was unearthed by
an excavator on Friday Nov 25th and detonated at 4.45 on Saturday afternoon- the
blast was felt as far away as Chesterfield & Sheffield.

Ahr Bomb

sight worth seeing, some of the weirdest clothing I shall ever see was on show, and this was only the men, 'I mean who wears their girdle on the outside of the dress?'). Sports days were held on the Juniors' sports field, this venue was ideal for the rule benders to perform in the egg and spoon race and the three legged race; football matches were staged between the ladies and the men of the village. These events would last for at least a month sometimes five or six weeks, I could go on forever.

The schools were also involved in sing-songs, plays, physical fitness shows by the boys, the girls performed too, but dare I say it, they were nearly as good as the boys. It can be said that the village came very close to the target maybe a few pounds short and that was some achievement for little Killamarsh. Contrary to what people would have us believe, each village would try its hardest to outdo the others, but in this case it was the best sort of rivalry.

The villages would also hold events to support the Royal Navy and the Merchant Navy, there were no such comments as I cannot afford it, everyone would have given their last penny and maybe some did.

What an example was set in those dark days, everyone in Killamarsh would pull together with only one result in mind: Victory no matter what the cost. This must be our small tribute to the ordinary people of the village for their fortitude and generosity especially in the days when there seemed to be no light at the end of the tunnel.

As the war years wore on things were going very wrong for Hitler and his armies in Europe and Russia. They were falling back on all fronts, so he decided to deploy his terror weapons. The first was the V1 or Flying Bomb, named Doodlebugs with typical British wit. You could hear them coming, it was when they fell silent that was the time to take cover. This machine was not piloted and once launched it flew automatically till at a certain point in its flight the engine would cut out and it fell to earth with a tremendous explosion. The southern counties of England suffered thousands of these bombs.

One Sunday morning in 1944 between 6am and 8am, one of these doodlebugs flew over Norwood in a westerly direction. After clearing the village the engine cut out and it crashed near the entrance to Cow Lane with an almighty bang, just clearing the LMS rail line. The explosion created a very large crater. It was reported that a fault must have occurred in its navigation system for it to have reached our village, but we asked ourselves, "had Hitler heard of our Buy a Spitfire weeks and was seeking revenge?"

The southern counties including London suffered an even more devastating weapon, The V2. This was a long range rocket which travelled faster than the speed of sound, therefore the rocket struck the ground and exploded before the sound of its flight caught up with it, so as a consequence no warning could be given.

At last the end of the war approached. Russian troops were on the outskirts of Berlin, the British and American armies were running amok all over the western side of Germany up to the river Oder. The ladies of the village were anticipating the end of the war so they started to gather the ingredients for the celebrations marking the end of hostilities. Of course all this had to be done without the children knowing anything about it, which in itself was a masterpiece of subterfuge the question must be raised just where did those ladies get the food from?

Then came that day in May 1945, peace in Europe at last. Prime Minister Winston Churchill said "the war in Europe is over so grant yourselves a few days celebration, and then the war in the Far East is to be decided" as Japan was still undefeated. So at last the ladies were able to organise street parties, there were two at Norwood, one at Highmoor and one in Jubilee Crescent.

The mothers as well as the children all had a wonderful time, most of the attendees at these parties will be all be senior citizens now, but we would like to hear from you and share any memories you have of those far off days.

Japan was finally overcome 4 months later in September and peace ruled the world, so we had another excuse to hold more and bigger parties.

13. Peace at Last

During all the celebrations the village was preparing to welcome our boys home, there was the need to construct houses for them and their families and also to create employment for them.

Before the men came home the council employed German and Italian prisoners of war to build roads and lay services, and also to assist in the erection of 'prefabs'. These were prefabricated houses manufactured in Sheffield, transported to the site in sections and put together by the prisoners under supervision. These houses were only intended as a stand-by and it was stated at the time, in 1946, that they would be replaced within ten years. They are still occupied and serviceable today in the year 2010, such is the quality of these buildings.

There was such a chronic housing shortage that some people from our village were forced to squat in the buildings that were once part of an anti-aircraft battery near Beighton until enough housing was available in Killamarsh.

The men returning home found it relatively easy to find work in the factories and construction sites, but many of them found it difficult to settle down. The old village ways had gone forever, the village they had left was gone and a strange one had taken its place.

Everyone was still rationed as to food and all other goods such as clothing and sweets. There were also shortages of cigarettes and of course fruit from abroad was still in short supply. While the queue outside the cinema stood waiting to get in, a wag would shout "Bananas at Mallenders" (a local fruit shop) in the vain hope that some people would leave the queue and they could move forward. No, it never worked.

These ladies organised the childrens party for Victory in Europe, May 1945.

In fact everyone had another five years of austerity to endure before the shops could stop asking for coupons for purchases. But never mind, we had the street lights back on and we did not have to worry about blackout regulations any more.

The Parish Council came to the fore now and occupied itself in getting some semblance of order to the letting of homes with the help and assistance of the District Council. Road signs which had been taken down to confuse the invaders at the start of the war had to be replaced; tank traps had to be removed and ARP warden posts were demolished. School air raid shelters were filled in and the area landscaped, and of course, the Anderson shelters taken to pieces. Some continued to be used for years, often as coalhouses. Our next door neighbours took the door off their shelter, filled it to ground level with water and kept fish in it for many years.

VE party, Norwood canteen, May 1945

Houses, so long neglected during the war, needed bringing up to a decent standard. But even progress on this was limited due to the acute shortage of materials, mainly timber, which had to be channelled to the big cities first to replace bombed properties and also to repair the damaged factories.

14. The Housing Boom in Killamarsh and the End of the Corner Shops

At the end of the Second World War the village was blessed with at least 50 shops situated at points all over the village selling all manner of goods from darning wool to cycles, groceries to suits and curtains. If a customer were to ask for a certain article in one shop and that shop did not have it, the shopkeeper would suggest that the customer try so-and-so as they may carry the article, such was the cohesion in the village in those days.

Then came the housing boom. No, not council homes this time, but private dwellings. Large swathes of older housing including many of the above-mentioned shops were demolished to accommodate these new homes. But sadly, hardly any shops were replaced to compensate for the numbers destroyed.

So began the erosion of the community spirit which had been so marked in Killamarsh. The same thing happened to other small towns and villages as people were more and more obliged to shop outside the village. Thus, denied the customers they needed to stay solvent, the corner shops just faded away.

In the 1950s the National Coal Board contracted Messers Henry Boot to construct sectional concrete houses for their employees, mostly for men working at Westthorpe Colliery. They were built in the Delves

Row of shops on Churchtown.
The church tower can be seen in the background.

on the west side of High Street to the rear of the old rectory. The next large estate to be built was the Wimpey houses, so-called after George Wimpey. This was a very large construction company responsible for many housing contracts countrywide in the 1950s and 60s.

The village was growing at great speed and as such its ways and traditions were disappearing as it approached township size. During the war Killamarsh Feast was not held because of the black-out regulations. When hostilities ended the Feast struggled on for a year or two, but the fairs ceased visiting due to lack of interest. The Summer Festival also ceased and the cinema closed through lack of support. This, I fear seems to have been the fate of so many villages over the years. The giant shopping malls have a lot to answer for regarding the loss of community spirit in villages such as Killamarsh. The question must be asked whether television contributed to this as well.

The worst thing to happen to our village (this has to be a personal opinion) was the loss of its green fields, buried under asphalt, bricks and mortar, never to be enjoyed by future generations. The overwhelming impression at the time was that the village would become a dormitory, somewhere for people to sleep in their homes then leave the village to go to work, shop and for their entertainment. So, in 1972, funding was obtained from several sources and a Leisure Centre was built to the rear of the Wagstaff villas on Sheffield Road, and also a library. The Leisure Centre boasted a large hall for functions such as wedding and birthday celebrations. There was a stage which could be used by anyone for music and performances such as the productions staged by 'Killamarsh Dreams'.

In 1983-84 the Sports Centre was introduced, with a multi-gym. Soon after the Cat-Gallows Bar followed and still later, in 2000, the Sports Hall came into being after National Lottery funding was obtained. It was hoped that this would lead residents to stay in the village and enjoy the local amendities regardless of whether they were old or young. The only drawback to all this work was the fact that Killamarsh could not have its own swimming baths. The authorities stated that the baths at Eckington were capable of accommodating swimmers from our village and that Eckington was only three miles away so there was no pressing need for baths in Killamarsh.

15. Killamarsh Today

As our village has roads leading to Sheffield and Chesterfield and is very close to the M1, at times Killamarsh suffers quite large volumes of mixed traffic. There are three schools in the village: St Giles Church of England School on Sheepcote Road, and the Infants and Junior Schools at Norwood. When pupils reach the age of eleven they are bussed to Eckington Comprehensive School to continue their education.

Killamarsh can boast a fantastic Medical Centre built on the site of the old cinema on Sheffield Road and accommodating five doctors, in all four males and one female GP. They are Dr A. Sutherland, Dr P. Cracknell, Dr S.R. Shaw, Dr G. Strachan and Dr Hena Brah. The Centre offers a vast range of services including family planning, maternity care, child health advice and minor surgery. Practice nurses provide for diabetes, blood pressure checks, wounds aftercare, influenza injections and immunisations for children. The health care in the village is second to none.

To resurrect the community spirit in the village we hold a village Cultural Festival annually, organised by the Community Trust who supply most of the finance for the project, assisted by Parish, District and County councils. The schools and the churches, Church of England and Nonconformist, are all involved in making this day something to remember. There have been three festivals to date and they were all a resounding success.

The church has come to the fore thanks to the vicar Reverend Helen Guest, who is extremely interested in reviving the community spirit and wishes to be involved in everything appertaining to this.

I can only hope that history will record that our spirit continued to strengthen throughout the years of the new millennium in our village of 'Chinewoldmaresc'. Everything seems to be moving in that direction; but that is for someone else to record in the future.

Epilogue

How does one finish writing the history of a vibrant village?

It is impossible, and history is still being made. The one thing we do not need is a war to create history. The birth of a baby is history to the family the child is born into, the building of a new housing estate, when a young family move into their first new home, these are the things that make history and should be recorded as such.

The building of a brand new footbridge over the River Rother and over the old LMS line between Killamarsh and Halfway is history in the making.

By the time this attempt at writing is published it will be under construction. What a boon this will be to the walkers, cyclists and horse riders as they will not have to take their lives into their hands as they do now when crossing by the present road bridge. We will close now and leave future history for someone else to record.

Thank you for your company in this endeavour.